BODYBUILDING 201

BODYBUILDING 201

EVERYTHING YOU NEED TO KNOW TO TAKE YOUR BODY TO THE NEXT LEVEL

ROBERT WOLFF, Ph.D.

Contemporary Books

Chicago New York San Francisco Lisbon London Madrid Mexico City
Milan New Delhi San Juan Seoul Singapore Sydney Toronto

Library of Congress Cataloging-in-Publication Data

Wolff, Robert, Ph.D.
    Bodybuilding 201 : everything you need to know to take your body to the next level /
Robert Wolff.
        p.   cm.
    Includes index.
    ISBN 0-07-141321-9
    1. Bodybuilding.   I. Title: Bodybuilding two hundred one.   II. Title.

GV546.5W66   2003
646.7′5—dc21   2003053084

1 2 3 4 5 6 7 8 9 0   VLP/VLP   2 1 0 9 8 7 6 5 4 3

ISBN 0-07-141321-9

Interior photographs by Ralph DeHaan Photography
Interior illustrations copyright © Ken Lain

McGraw-Hill books are available at special quantity discounts to use as premiums and sales promotions, or for use in corporate training programs. For more information, please write to the Director of Special Sales, Professional Publishing, McGraw-Hill, Two Penn Plaza, New York, NY 10121-2298. Or contact your local bookstore.

This book is printed on acid-free paper.

CONTENTS

by Joe Weider

The book you're about to read is written by the man I consider to be one of the best and most knowledgeable people in all of bodybuilding and fitness. His grasp, understanding, writing, and teaching of bodybuilding, my Weider Principles, and his highly motivating style is second to none. Bob Wolff is a top expert on the Weider System and Principles that all the bodybuilders and champions use, and if you follow his advice, you're virtually guaranteed to develop a great body.

People have often asked how I met Bob. I'd like to tell you the story of how it all began.

Some years ago, a young man came to see me. I don't think he realized it at the time, but I saw something in him he didn't see. Call it a gut feeling or a hunch, but there was something about him that was different, what I believed to be an untapped ability. So I decided I'd put him to the test.

"Can you write?" I asked him, as I studied the expression on his face.

"I don't know," he replied with a surprised look. "I can write letters."

"Good. I want you to write something for me."

"What should I write about?" he asked.

"Write about anything you want. Let me see what you can do."

And with that, the young man left.

A week later, my secretary paged me and said that the young man I had met a week earlier had come back and wanted to see me. As he was escorted into my office, I asked him to sit down, and as he did, he handed me a stapled stack of handwritten words on yellow legal paper.

"Mr. Weider," he said, "I've written something for you, and I hope you like it."

I took the paper, handed it back to him, and asked him to put his telephone number on the top of the front page. I told him I'd read it and let him know what I thought.

Three days later, I called his home, spoke to his mother, and told her to give her son the message to call me. The next day he did, and this is what I told him.

"I've read your article ("How to Stay Motivated to Work Out") and I love it. Now, I'm going to tell you three things, so listen closely. Number one: I want to give you a monthly column in *Muscle & Fitness*. Number two: I want you to write for all of my magazines. And number three: You've got a full-time job working for me out here in California anytime you like."

That young man's name is Bob Wolff.

Since that time, I have shared many laughs and happy times with Bob. We've worked on great articles together. We've had many discussions over lunch and dinner about anything from history to religion, bodybuilding to business. I've sent him all over the world to talk to, interview, and work with many of the world's greatest names in bodybuilding, fitness, and health. He has written books with bodybuilding's greatest bodybuilders and has covered bodybuilding's biggest events, whether they were in China, Finland, Austria, Korea, or anywhere else.

And even though he left the magazine some years ago to become an author, the one thing he has always stayed true to—and I believe always will—is a genuine love for training and staying hungry to learn new and different things, the very things that can help you.

I see a lot of myself in Bob. Perhaps that was one of the things that drew me to him from the start. He's a man of great talents: bodybuilding, writing, music, speaking, and many other things the world has yet to see. And I'm proud of him.

As I think back on the more than 70 years I've lived and loved weight training and working out, it amazes me to this day that I still have the same passion for it that I did as a young boy in Canada. A young boy who trained hard and was excited with every new inch of muscle I put on my body and every 10 pounds of strength I'd gain on the barbell. Sure, I'm older, but the passion is still there, and it can be there for you, too, if you live a healthy life, work out, have faith in yourself, use your God-given talents, and find just the right kind of balance in everything you do.

Time changes all of us. Youth leaves us, and in its place come knowledge, wisdom, understanding, and the capacity to enjoy the gift of life, appreciate good health, treasure new experiences, remember back on great ones, and cherish good friends.

Bob Wolff is such a friend. He changed many people's lives when he wrote for my magazines. And I'm happy to say, with this new book, *Bodybuilding 201*, he can do the same for you.

With every best wish,
Joe Weider

ACKNOWLEDGMENTS

I want to give my sincere thanks to those who are a part of this book.

To Joe Weider: Thank you, Joe, for being my good friend and my mentor, and for seeing something in me I never saw. I will always cherish the lessons you taught me and the time we spent together.

To Matthew Carnicelli: I want to thank you and everyone at Contemporary Books for making this book a reality.

To Ralph DeHaan: It was great to work with my magazine photographer buddy again. Thanks for the wonderful pictures. And special thanks to models Candice Michelle and Chad Moston.

To Ken Lain: So great to hook up with you after all these years. Thank you, Ken, for the inspiration and advice that's going to help a lot of people.

To Christian Finn: Many thanks, Christian, for the terrific research.

To Dr. Jeffrey Halbrecht: I greatly appreciate your expertise and knowledge. Thank you for sharing it with so many.

To Carol Semple: Carol, you are the epitome of brains, beauty, elegance, and class. You were the woman who took fitness competition to the next level and raised the bar for all who will come after you. Thank you for being such a wonderful friend all these years.

To Ronnie Coleman: Thank you for your words and friendship. Ronnie, you could win 10 more Mr. Olympia titles and you'd always be the humble, friendly, and good person you are, and for that, I say thank you with much admiration.

And to you, my reader friend: It's because of you that I write, and it's because of you and your kind words and support that I'll keep writing, I hope, many more books that can touch your life and help you. I never forget who buys and reads my books, and to all of you I say thank you.

May you always be happy, healthy, and blessed.

INTRODUCTION

First of all, I'd like to thank all of you who have made *Bodybuilding 101* so popular. I'm happy to have received so many letters and E-mails from people all over the world who told me how the book helped them reach their fitness goals. Always remember: the credit goes to you for making it happen. You're the one who made it work for you; all I did was give you some information.

So where do we go after *Bodybuilding 101*? It would be easy to answer this question if there were a new set of exercises you could graduate to after you had mastered the basics, but only a handful of variations exist for any of them.

Take squats. You can do front squats, back squats, hack squats, Smith machine squats, deep squats, partial-rep squats, dead-stop squats, barbell squats, dumbbell squats, or no-weight/bodyweight squats. While all of these are squat variations, they're simply different ways of doing one thing: going up and down. A squat.

This applies to exercises for nearly any bodypart you can imagine. There are lots of variations and ways to do an exercise, yet the mechanics of doing it—the start-to-finish movement—rarely change. You can go up and down, backward and forward, side to side, or a combination of the three, but any exercise and movement of the body will always be in these planes of motion.

Many years ago, when Europeans and Americans did groundbreaking work to discover and refine new ways to use resistance to exercise the body, a golden age of exercise was born. It could be argued that more discoveries about exercise and how to train the body were made in that brief period of time than in any time before or after. Although little was known about how to apply these findings to the body, the basic model of how the body responds to resistance and progressive resistance has remained the foundation of modern exercise practice.

Along the way, machines to work the body have been devised, developed, and implemented. Some of them have been good and are still used today. Others were gimmicks, all show and no go. In some ways, little has changed. Just look at some of the devices you see on TV infomercials.

But regardless of how big or small, expensive or cheap, fancy or plain a machine is, there's still no better way to strengthen, tone, and shape your body than with resistance training using barbells and dumbbells. If barbells and dumbbells are all you've got, then rest assured that's all you'll ever need.

If you're like the many men and women who have written to me, you want to know other ways you can train your body, to make it stronger and bigger, leaner and shapelier. You want to know how you can eat better. You want to learn more about science and your body, including ways to prevent injuries and accelerate healing from injuries. You want to tap into the power of your brain and use it to motivate you more effectively, control your thoughts, and direct those thoughts to helping you build a better-looking and better-feeling body.

To all of you, I present *Bodybuilding 201: Everything You Need to Know to Take Your Body to the Next Level*.

In *Bodybuilding 201* we're going to talk about all of these things and more. But be warned: if you're looking for the quick fix—the miracle exercise or food or supplement, or lots of hype and promises—then it's time to take this book back to the store and get your money back, because you won't find what you're looking for in these pages.

But if you're looking for some tips and ideas that are *real world* and will give you some *real results*, then hold on to this book, because what you're about to learn can help you big time.

Enough talk. We've got some learning to do, a body to change, and a lot of fun to have!

PART 1

A New Look at Fundamentals

1

Staying Motivated

Remember this simple formula, given in order of importance:

- If you think right, you'll eat right.
- If you eat right, you'll have the energy to train right.
- If you train right, you'll have the physical stimulus to change how your body looks and feels in all the right ways.

Now, here's how to understand the formula:

- **Using your brain:** You've got to think right before you'll take an action.
- **Using your food:** You've got to eat right before you'll have the energy to exercise and the ability to change how you look and feel.
- **Using your body:** You've got to think right to be motivated to exercise, give your brain a target to shoot for, eat well to change your body's composition, and be energized to exercise to shape and build your muscles to your body's genetic potential.

IT'S SIMPLE

You can buy and take all the supplements you can afford. You can have the best workout imaginable. You can get just the right amount of sleep. But if your mental game is off, you'll get only a fraction of the results you'll get when your brain and body are in sync.

Far too many bodybuilders lack mental strategies and direction for their training time and energy. They want to "train hard" or "get big" or "get ripped" or "lean down" or "get strong" or whatever. But when asked how they are going to achieve those goals, many are clueless. They'll work out harder, longer, or more intensely, or follow the latest stars' routines, or try the latest supplement they see hyped up in magazines, or do anything else they think will give them the edge and get them to their goal as quickly as possible.

They are like little robots with only a few instructions to follow— "Must train harder," "Must get bigger and stronger"—and they arrange their lives and schedules so that week after week they do the same things over and over that they believe they must do to reach those goals.

But it never ends. The majority of them never quite reach that goal—some because of wrong training and nutrition, and the majority because of their genetic limitations—and they get more frustrated at the lack of progress and push their bodies until their bodies just say, "I've had enough of this nonsense: time for an injury." Kaboom!

YOUR ANSWER CAN CHANGE EVERYTHING

There are more people whose workouts are controlled by their body image than there are people whose workouts control their body image. Let me say that another way: if how you look controls what you think and what you do, you'll constantly be unhappy. So which one are you?

Look back on every exercise you've ever done. Think of every workout you've ever had. Try to remember everything you've ever eaten. You'll discover that the way you look and feel right now is a result of your thoughts about what you should and should not do; those thoughts directed the actions you took.

Your thinking makes your life. You are the director and star of your life movie, and you are the one who will either make it happen or keep it from happening. No one else: just you, my friend.

No one keeps you going to that gym but you. No one forces you to eat the way you do but you. No one gives you the desire to be bigger, stronger, and leaner, or anything else you want, but you. So if you are the one who thinks the thoughts, who accepts the beliefs, and who takes the action that

makes all these things happen, how much more incredible could your life be if you finally took control of your thinking and directed it in ways that can *help* you instead of hold you back?

Always remember that you are a brain with a body. The body is only your transport vehicle while you're living on this earth, a means to get you where you want to go or help you do what you want to do. Your body doesn't think. Its job is to listen to the directions it gets from your brain. If your thinking is right, then everything else in your life—including your body—will be right. Change your thinking and you'll change your body and life.

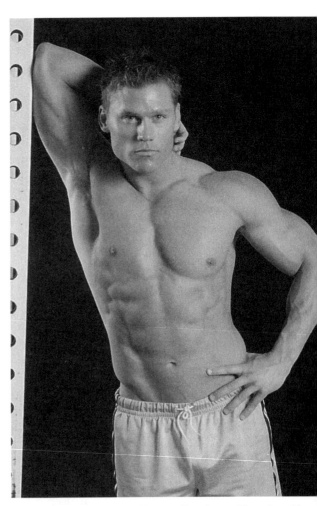

Here's a secret for you: taking small actions will produce big results if you just stay with it. Soon, you will achieve the body you want.

FINDING REASONS TO STAY MOTIVATED AND KEEP TRAINING

Staying motivated to work out month after month is very tough for a lot of people. Many people work out because of guilt or fear: they don't want to get fat or get sick. Others do it because of peer pressure or relationships. Some do it to hide pain and frustration: perhaps an eating disorder, poor body image or self-esteem, or unresolved life situations that they keep avoiding.

Yet many work out to look and feel great and for all the right reasons. They know that strength comes and goes, as do youth and looks, but looking and feeling their best—at whatever age—can be enjoyed at any time. They also understand that anything that takes away from the enjoyment of working out—such as pushing themselves and their bodies too hard or too often, or other obsessive behaviors—only zaps motivation.

Any time working out becomes something you dread or get nervous about, that's the time you should quit. It might be for a few days or even a few weeks, but your brain and body are telling you something very important—and it's critical that you listen and learn the message.

Working out is something you do *for* your body, not *to* it. And that's the discovery that will keep you motivated. Doing something *for* your body makes you feel good. It's enjoyable and healthy, recharges you, and keeps the desire burning inside you to look forward to doing it again.

Doing something *to* your body makes it feel stressed, pushed, and overloaded. From insanely intense workouts month after month, to popping supplements that are overpriced and ineffective, to being so busy that it's hard to find 15 minutes a day to sit quietly and read or think—focusing on doing something *to* your body will keep you from enjoying the gift of exercise and all its benefits.

One of the keys to staying motivated is having something to look forward to. Life is exciting in proportion to the number of things you have to look forward to. And you'll find it far easier to stay and keep motivated if you have enough reasons and rewards for doing the things you do.

We like gifts and surprises, and reasons and rewards for your actions are like little gifts and surprises you give to yourself each day. Once you change your motivation for training from wanting "to get big and cut" to wanting to feel good, you're on the right path to maintaining that motiva-

tion and receiving those gifts and surprises.

You may ask, "What if being big and cut makes me feel good?" If it does, it'll last only a brief time. The amount of time, work, and money it will take to keep that artificial good feeling will quickly give way to "C'mon, you need to push harder," and very soon you'll be burned out, injured, or both.

The longer I train and the more I observe all kinds of people who train—from beginners to Mr. Olympias—the more I'm convinced that maintaining the kind of training intensity needed to stay massive, or keep getting massive, is not only incredibly difficult but a tremendous strain on the body.

When guys like Steve Reeves and John Grimek were world champions, they trained very hard and very intelligently, and in street clothes they looked like regular guys who had a nice physique. They also looked like that on *any* day of the week. They didn't buy into this bigger-is-always-best mentality. They enjoyed life, yet training wasn't their life. They had other motivations and interests, and training was simply a part of the big picture they called life.

And that's what helped them stay motivated. Training helped them look and feel great. It gave them the strength, flexibility, and endurance to do all the other things in their lives that much better and with greater ease. And because their brains associated such enjoyment and benefit with training, this kept the training fire going—for more than 50 years, for the rest of their lives.

And these are only two of the countless numbers of people who have discovered the same thing. Joe Weider, who is over 80 years old, still goes to the office and works out every morning. He doesn't have to do that. He doesn't need to do it. He does it because it makes him feel good, keeps him feeling good, strengthens his mind and body, and helps him do all the other things in his life. He'll train for the rest of his life.

Look at all the reasons why you're working out right now. Keep the ones that will be good for you 5, 10, 15, and 20 years from now, and get rid of all the rest. Your training and your life will be transformed.

RESEARCH UPDATE: STAYING FIT

Six months after starting an aerobic exercise program, 5 out of 10 people give up, claiming they simply don't have the time to train regularly. However, most people aren't aware that it takes far less aerobic exercise to *maintain* your fitness than it does to *increase* it. Some evidence that this is the case comes from a study published in *Medicine and Science in Sports and Exercise.**

Aerobic Exercise

A group of 12 subjects took part in a program of regular aerobic exercise. The program involved cycling and running for 40 minutes, six days each week. The average increase in aerobic fitness after 10 weeks of training was 20 to 25 percent. Subjects were then placed in one of two groups and continued to exercise for a further 15 weeks. The first group trained at the same intensity and duration four days each week; the second group trained at the same intensity and duration only two days each week.

The researchers found that aerobic capacity—a marker of aerobic fitness—remained the same in both groups, despite the fact that the second group was training only twice each week. In short, the frequency of aerobic exercise needed to maintain fitness is less than that required to improve it.

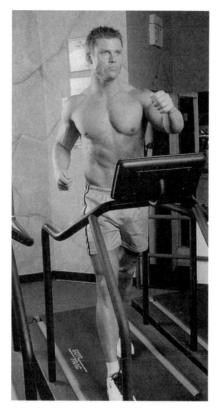

Adding some type of aerobic program will help you reach the body and level of fitness you want that much quicker.

Work or family commitments might be stopping you from training as often as you'd like. If so, don't cut out exercise completely. Aerobic fitness is easily lost in a matter of weeks. In fact, if you were to spend the next 20 days in bed doing nothing, your aerobic capacity would drop more than 20 percent.

Frequency

Two days a week of aerobic exercise might not seem like enough. And if you're trying to lose weight, it probably isn't. However, this study shows that training twice each week is sufficient to maintain your aerobic fitness. Although these findings are important for busy people who want to get fit and stay that way, you can also use them to design an effective training program.

Let's say, for example, that you're happy with your current level of fitness and you want to focus on other goals, such as gaining strength. Unfortunately, the problem with trying to do everything at once is that you run the risk of overtraining. By varying the frequency of your workouts (an example is shown in Table 1) you can gain strength and maintain your fitness level without spending hours in the gym.

TABLE 1: Variations in Training Frequency According to Goal

Goal	Aerobic exercise	Strength training
Increase aerobic capacity	4× per week	1× per week
Increase strength	2× per week	3× per week

Varying your training program every three to six weeks is also a great way to keep it interesting, and it helps prevent the boredom that can sap your motivation.

* Hickson, R. C., and M. A. Rosenkoetter. "Reduced Training Frequencies and Maintenance of Increased Aerobic Power." *Medicine and Science in Sports and Exercise* 13 (1981): 13–16.

2

Respecting Your Body

Since the book *Bodybuilding 101* was published, I have been surprised by the number of people who've written to me asking for more information on injuries, particularly treatment options and prevention tips. I've been equally surprised by the number of people who have injuries—many as a result of doing too much exercise, or lifting too much weight for too long, or exercising incorrectly.

So I asked one of the top sports orthopedic surgeons in the United States, Dr. Jeffrey Halbrecht, medical director of The Institute for Arthroscopy and Sports Medicine in San Francisco, to discuss the four biggest injury problem areas for athletes—the shoulder, elbow, knee, and ankle—and the best treatments and rehabilitations for them.

Dr. Halbrecht also has some interesting observations about female athletes and unique factors they should consider when weight training or when involved in other sports. You can read more in-depth information about injuries from Dr. Halbrecht in Appendix A.

Meanwhile, later in this book I'm going to give you five great ways to stretch and show you some tried-and-true effective stretches for the major muscle groups, as well as exercises you can do to help you recover from an injury and keep you strong.

The best ways to prevent any weight training injury include the following:

- Warm up properly.
- Don't overdo it.
- Exercise with excellent form.
- Give your body plenty of rest and recuperation.
- Stop immediately at the first sign of pain.

THE IMPORTANCE OF NONTRAINING DAYS

Let's talk a little about days off. When you're getting great results from working out, it's easy to get excited and push yourself a little harder in your zeal to keep it going. But you've got to be careful. Just as too little exercise won't stimulate your muscles to grow, too much won't either. It's much better to not do enough than to do too much.

Most beginners achieve growth spurts unparalleled by advanced body-builders: their bodies seem to grow overnight. Many beginners are also resilient to overtraining; they can push themselves into what would normally be the overtraining zone and their bodies will adapt to those demands by growing and getting stronger very quickly.

If only it could last! But it doesn't. Soon the phenomenal growth rate slows down and the beginning body-builder enters the "more-intensity-for-any-growth" zone. That's why you need to give your body plenty of rest—especially if it's still sore from the last workout—to keep it fresh and growing. *Never train a bodypart that's still sore from your last workout.*

By all means, stretch out and get blood flowing into the sore muscle area, but don't train that bodypart until it has fully recovered, and don't throw in an extra day of training just because you want your body to grow faster. It won't. If you're on a Monday-Wednesday-Friday program, take those remaining four days off for rest. *And take one complete week off from working out for every six to eight weeks of consistent training.*

PAINKILLERS AND MUSCLE GROWTH

Over-the-counter painkillers (such as ibuprofen) are a popular way to ease the pain and soreness that manifest 24 to 48 hours after a tough workout. However, what most people don't real-ize is that high doses of these pain-killers can put the brakes on muscle growth by blunting the normal rise in protein synthesis that occurs after exercise.

Protein synthesis is one important factor controlling the rate of muscle growth. In simple terms, your muscles grow larger when protein synthesis is greater than protein breakdown. If you think of your muscles as a bath, pro-tein synthesis is like water coming into the bath; protein breakdown is like water being drained from the bath. When there's more water coming into the bath than there is going out, you get bigger muscles.

One of the ways that painkillers work is to suppress the synthesis of substances known as prostaglandins. These very same prostaglandins have a profound effect on muscle growth. Some evidence linking prostaglandins to a reduced rate of protein synthesis comes from a trial published in the *Journal of Clinical Endocrinology and Metabolism.*[1] A group of male subjects with an average age of 25 were assigned to one of three groups. All groups performed 10 to 14 sets of 10 eccentric (that is, with emphasis on the lowering part of the rep) repetitions for the muscles on the front of the thigh.

After completing the workout, group one received the maximal over-the-counter dose of ibuprofen (1,200 milligrams daily). Group two was given acetaminophen (4,000 milligrams daily). The third group received a placebo, which contained no active ingredients.

When muscle samples were analyzed 24 hours after exercise, levels of a prostaglandin called PGF2 increased by an average of 77 percent in the group using the placebo. This

---

1 Trappe, T. A., J. D. Fluckey, F. White, C. P. Lambert, and W. J. Evans. "Skeletal Muscle PGF(2)(alpha) and PGE(2) in Response to Eccentric Resistance Exercise: Influence of Ibuprofen Acetaminophen." *Journal of Clinical Endocrinology and Metabolism* 86 (2001): 5067–70.

represents the normal response to exercise. However, PGF2 levels dropped by 1 percent and 14 percent in the ibuprofen and acetaminophen groups, respectively.

This was only a short-term study. The extent to which the prolonged use of painkillers affects muscle growth over a period of several weeks or months is open to debate. Although the occasional use of painkillers isn't likely to cause a problem, it's generally best to avoid them.

If you do want to prevent postexercise soreness, the best way is simply to ease your way into a new training program gradually. Even stretching, commonly recommended as a way to reduce delayed-onset muscle soreness (also known as DOMS) has very little effect on the pain and soreness you feel after exercise.

FORCED REST BREAKS

So if you, as an advanced *Bodybuilding 201* athlete, can now generate greater power and intensity much more quickly, then your workouts should be better and take less time. The question is, what do you do with all that "free time" away from the gym? Rest and enjoy your life!

RESEARCH UPDATE: The Link Between Sleep and Body Fat

A Spanish research team has shown a link between body fat and the amount of time you spend sleeping. Analyzing a group of 814 men and 958 women from the Mediterranean area of Spain, the authors found that people who slept for more than nine hours each day were *less* likely to be overweight than those sleeping for six hours or less.

Based on their findings, the authors concluded that the odds of obesity are 24 percent lower for each additional hour you spend asleep. (Interestingly, but not surprisingly, results also showed that people watching TV for more than four hours each day were more likely to be obese than those watching TV for less than one hour. The odds of obesity are 30 percent higher for each hour you spend in front of the TV.)

One possible explanation for the link between body fat and sleep is the rise in insulin resistance commonly seen in people deprived of sleep. Other studies show that sleep deprivation, even for as little as 24 hours, can lead to signs of insulin resistance.

What Is Insulin Resistance?

Insulin is a hormone that helps to transport nutrients (such as carbohydrate) from your blood into body tissues (such as muscle or fat). Contrary to popular belief, insulin doesn't make you fat. Rather, it promotes a metabolic environment that encourages the storage of fat. Insulin increases the activity of lipoprotein lipase, an enzyme that promotes fat storage. Insulin also inhibits the action of hormone-sensitive lipase, an enzyme responsible for the mobilization of free fatty acids. Insulin resistance, in simple terms, means that the ability of insulin to dispose of glucose in the liver and other tissues is reduced.

Think of it this way. If you tan very easily when exposed to a lot of sunlight, you could be called sun sensitive. But if you need more exposure to the sun to produce the same effect, you could be considered sun resistant. Someone who is sun resistant would need to spend more time in the sun to get tanned than one who is sun sensitive. In the same way, some people are resistant to the effects of insulin and produce more insulin than those who are insulin sensitive.

Why does insulin resistance matter? Scientists point to insulin resistance as the trigger for a host of health problems, including obesity, cardiovascular disease, and type 2 diabetes. Insulin resistance is the cumulative effect of poor eating and lifestyle habits. In fact, in some studies rats have shown signs of insulin resistance after just two weeks on a high-fat, high-sugar diet.

The Bottom Line

This research shouldn't be taken to imply that sleeping fewer than six hours each night is a guarantee that you'll put on weight. After all, everyone can tolerate different amounts of sleep. It's also important to note that the effects of sleep deprivation on insulin levels can be partially offset by physical activity. What's most important is recognizing that a healthy lifestyle involves balancing work and rest in a way that suits you. Getting sufficient sleep is just as important as eating right and exercising correctly.

The greater physiological demands of increased training intensity require that you give your body more rest. Hard workouts tax your central nervous system, along with your muscles and connective tissue. World-record bench presser Ken Lain, who has bench pressed over 700 pounds, once told me that his body needed 21 days to recover after an all-out lift. Three weeks!

And I know some weight trainers who think they're ready to hit the iron and work the same bodypart again two days after a hard workout. "I'll lose strength and get small," they tell me.

Not so. The truth is, *they'll get small and lose strength because they haven't allowed enough time for recovery.*

I caution you not to wait until you stop growing or stop getting stronger or sustain an injury before you take a layoff. Take an extra day off from training any time your body is still sore from a previous workout. And take a complete week off from training every six to eight weeks. You will not get weak or out of shape. Remember: you control your body. Your body doesn't control you unless you give it that power.

RESEARCH UPDATE: The Truth About Creatine and Endurance

New research shows that the diet supplement creatine could improve your performance in the latter stages of sports such as field hockey, soccer, or football. While the benefits of creatine have been shown during short periods (less than 10 minutes) of exercise, what's not so clear is whether these improvements persist throughout the middle and latter stages of exercise. So a research team from the University of Western Australia decided to find out.

They took a group of active (but not well-trained) men and asked them to perform a series of all-out bike sprints for 80 minutes. The sprints were separated by recovery periods that varied in duration. This exercise test was designed to mimic the demands of sports such as soccer or field hockey. After completing the test, the men were split into two groups. One group took 20 grams of creatine daily, while the others were given a placebo. Five days later, the men took the test again.

Creatine Improves Performance

Results showed that the total amount of work performed increased by 6 percent in the creatine group. No such improvements were found in subjects using the placebo. Moreover, the creatine group outperformed their colleagues in the middle and latter stages of the exercise test. Because the test was designed to mimic the demands of a sport involving repeated sprints (such as soccer or field hockey), the authors concluded that "the use of creatine supplementation for enhancing physical performance in multiple sprint sports (performed over a similar time frame) seems justified."*

That said, it's worth pointing out that there is evidence to show creatine may impair performance during endurance exercise. When cross-country runners used creatine, their times actually got worse. It seems that the weight gain that accompanies creatine supplementation may actually slow you down during certain sports or activities.

The Bottom Line

Creatine can enhance your performance during short, repeated bouts of high-intensity exercise—even when they're performed in the middle and latter stages of a match or training session. Traditionally, the use of creatine involves a "loading" phase. This involves consuming roughly 20 grams of creatine daily for up to five days. Loading with creatine also leads to a weight gain of several pounds.

An alternative method might be to use just 5 grams of creatine daily. This has been shown to "saturate" your muscles with creatine to the same degree as a loading phase, but it takes a little longer (30 days). Because you'll also gain weight more slowly, the 30-day protocol might give your body time to adapt to the small gain in weight and reduce the risk that creatine could interfere with your performance.

* Preen, D., B. Dawson, C. Goodman, S. Lawrence, and J. Beilby. "Effect of Creatine Loading on Long-Term Sprint Exercise Performance and Metabolism." *Medicine and Science in Sports and Exercise* 33 (2001): 814–21.

3

The No-Nonsense Nutrition Plan That Works

The immense popularity of diet books leaves little doubt that people will buy or read anything they think will give them "the answer" that will solve their weight loss problems. I see the same thing in bodybuilding. The magazines are full of "special four-page ad reports" that show before and after photos and stories of how a male or female went from fat to fabulous simply by using the advertised supplement.

And you know what? So many people are buying into that each month that these companies are making a killing. I read recently that one major fitness magazine takes in more than $40 million a year in advertising revenue—and most of it comes from supplement companies. And that's just one magazine; many of these supplement companies advertise in many magazines each month. I can tell you that those big full-page color ads each month are not cheap, so you gotta know someone is making lots of money. The question is, are they getting rich off you?

It's time you saved your money. But be warned: what I'm going to tell you about how to eat to be *naturally* big and *naturally* strong is going to be so boring, so unexciting that it will work wonders for you! What you're about to read is a description of what I did to put on 65 pounds of muscle in just two years. I did it by eating home cooking and protein shakes.

See, I told you it wasn't exciting, but looking for excitement in a can or bottle costs you a lot of money and won't get you the results you'll get—and keep—doing it this way.

Here's what I did:

1. I always ate a good breakfast that was typically either eggs (with the yolks) with a piece of wheat toast and juice, or raisin bran cereal with 2 percent milk and juice.
2. I had a mid-morning snack—either a bagel or a piece of fruit.
3. I had a nice lunch with lots of protein from beef, chicken, turkey, or fish, perhaps a small salad with Thousand Island dressing (not the nonfat variety).
4. I had a preworkout snack about 3:00 P.M.—either a banana or an apple.

5. I worked out about 3:30 P.M.
6. I had a dinner each night about 5:00 that would include any of the following meals:
   - Roast, vegetables, fruit salad
   - Spaghetti with meat sauce and parmesan cheese, salad, fruit
   - Fried chicken, green vegetables, fruit
   - Hamburger, French fries, fruit
   - Sloppy Joe, salad, fruit
   - Baked fish, vegetable, fruit
   - Pork chops, baked potato, fruit
   - Homemade vegetable soup with stew meat, deviled eggs, salad, fruit
   - Toasted cheese sandwich, sweet pickles, fruit salad
   - Chipped beef on toast, mashed potatoes, string beans, fruit
   - Meatloaf, mashed potatoes, tomato gravy, green beans, fruit
   - Broiled pork or beef shoulder, browned potato wedges, carrots, onions, fruit
   - Chili with cheese and crackers, salad, pudding or fruit
   - Fried shrimp with ketchup or cocktail sauce, fresh salad with Catalina or Thousand Island dressing, pudding
   - Salmon croquettes with peas, green beans, or salad, and fruit cocktail
   - Tuna salad, cottage fries, fruit
   - Liver with onions, mashed potatoes and gravy, string beans, fruit
   - Chicken salad, cottage fries, fruit
   - Homemade vegetable soup, celery stuffed with pimiento cheese, fruit
   - Tacos with beef or chicken, cheddar cheese, onion, tomato, lettuce, and hot sauce, and fruit salad
   - Pizza, tossed salad with Thousand Island, Catalina, or ranch dressing, fruit
   - Sliced turkey, mashed potatoes and gravy, fruit
   - Broiled chicken breast, baked potato, fruit
   - Fried chicken, mashed potatoes, spinach, fruit salad
   - Broiled steak, vegetable, fruit
   - Barbecued pork steaks, beans, fruit
   - Roast beef sandwich, tossed salad, fruit
   - Chicken stir-fry with frozen vegetables, soy sauce, and chow mein noodles, and pudding
7. About 8:00 each night, I'd have a milk and egg protein powder shake I'd make in a blender (the kind I always bought was Rheo Blair's Protein Powder). The shake contained:
   - 8 to 10 ounces of 2 percent milk
   - 2 to 3 scoops of protein powder
   - 1 raw egg (run under hot water for 30 to 60 seconds)
   - 1 or 2 scoops of ice cream

   I blended this mixture for 30 to 45 seconds or until it was the consistency I liked.
8. About 9:30 or 10:00 each night, I'd have a snack (about an hour before my bedtime), either regular cottage cheese mixed with pineapple, applesauce, peaches, or fruit cocktail, or a peanut butter and jelly sandwich on whole wheat bread with a glass of milk.
9. I always drank plenty of water throughout the day and with each meal.

Nothing exciting about that, eh? But take a good look at what I was doing without even realizing it.

- I ate a wide variety of foods that included lots of protein, moderate amounts of vegetable and fruit carbohydrates, and relatively small amounts of fat.
- My body was constantly fed and watered throughout the entire day

and night. Never did I experience the intense highs and lows of too much or not enough blood sugar. My energy level was always steady, stable, and predictable.

- I had plenty of energy for my workouts, so I was able to train long (if I wanted) and very hard.
- I refueled my muscles and body within 30 minutes after my workouts. I'd typically be in the gym at 3:15 or so, on the way home by 4:30, and back home at 5:00, where dinner was ready. (Thanks, Mom!)
- My body always had plenty of carbs for energy and protein for growth, repair, and recuperation.
- I rarely ate refined and processed carbs (like candy and junk food).
- Saturday was always my junk food day. I'd eat anything I wanted without worrying about whether it was "bad"—chips, dips, pizza, cookies, you name it. No limits on calories or quantity: I ate whatever I wanted. This completely satisfied my weekly craving for those foods, and I didn't want to eat them again for another week.
- I always ate more protein and calories on any days my body felt sore from the previous day's workout. Then I'd reduce my calories and protein back to normal levels as my body became less sore.
- With few exceptions, I ate at the same times, ate the same foods, and went to bed at the same times. Very predictable. Very effective.

If you're serious about doing it right and doing it naturally, then I'll tell you right now that what I did worked well and continues to work for me, more than 20 years later. I highly recommend that you give my eating plan a try. I think you and your body will absolutely love it!

LOSING FAT WHILE BUILDING MUSCLE

A common goal for many people who train, especially beginners, is to lose fat and build muscle at the same time. Trying to lose fat and build muscle simultaneously is difficult (but not impossible) because these goals put opposing demands on your body. To build new muscle tissue, your body needs energy. In other words, you'll need to overfeed—to consume *more* calories than you're burning each day. To lose fat, you need to create an energy deficit—to consume *fewer* calories than you burn.

Build Muscle
Of course, it is possible to lose fat and build muscle at the same time, especially if you're just starting an exercise program. But your progress will be a lot slower than if you were to devote all your energy to one goal—so slow, in fact, that it's easy to become discouraged by your lack of progress and throw in the towel.

The fact is, you're far more likely to get better results by splitting your training goals into several phases and working on one after the other. The hard part is deciding which goal to work toward first. The typical approach is to bulk up as quickly as possible by eating everything in sight. Then you simply shed the fat to reveal the layers of new muscle tissue you've worked so hard to build.

However, Dr. Gilbert Forbes, professor emeritus of pediatrics and biophysics at New York's University of Rochester, points out that during a period of overfeeding, you'll gain *more* muscle and *less* fat if you're already lean. In other words, if you want to lose fat and build muscle, focus on losing the fat first.[1]

---

1 Forbes, G. B. "Body Fat Content Influences the Body Composition Response to Nutrition and Exercise." *Annals of the New York Academy of Sciences* 904 (2000): 359–65.

Lose Fat

Fat is simply stored energy. Energy is neither created nor destroyed over time. Although it might change form, the total always remains the same. For example, the *chemical* energy in gasoline is changed into the same amount of *movement* energy in a moving car. When you put the brakes on, this movement energy isn't lost. Rather, it's converted into *heat* energy in the brakes.

The same principle holds true for the food you eat. Green plants use carbon dioxide, water, and energy from the sun to form a type of sugar called glucose. That's where the word *carbohydrate* comes from. *Carbo* means "carbon," while *hydrate* means "water." When you eat the plant (or the animal that has eaten the plant), the energy then is stored in your body in the form of fat, carbohydrate, or protein. When you exercise, this chemical energy is converted into both movement and heat energy.

OVERFEEDING

When you overfeed for a period of several weeks, it's common to gain a small amount of muscle as well as fat. In fact, obese people are not just over-

RESEARCH UPDATE:
Alcohol Calories

According to conventional wisdom, the infamous "beer belly" is caused by excess alcohol calories being stored as fat. However, researchers from the University of California have shown that less than 5 percent of the alcohol calories you consume are turned into fat. Rather, the main effect of alcohol is to reduce the amount of fat your body burns for energy. Successful weight loss is all about oxidizing (or burning) more calories than you eat. When they go on a diet, many people choose low-calorie alcoholic drinks, mainly because they contain fewer alcohol calories than their regular counterparts. However, a recent study published in the *American Journal of Clinical Nutrition* shows that even a very small amount of alcohol has a large impact on fat metabolism.*

Eight men were given two drinks of vodka and lemonade separated by 30 minutes. Each drink contained just under 90 calories. Fat metabolism was measured before and after consumption of the drink. For several hours after drinking the vodka, whole body lipid oxidation (a measure of how much fat your body is burning) dropped by a massive 73 percent.

Here's why. Rather than being stored as fat, the main fate of alcohol is conversion into a substance called acetate. In fact, blood levels of acetate after drinking the vodka were 2.5 times higher than normal. And it appears this sharp rise in acetate puts the brakes on fat loss.

A car engine typically uses only one source of fuel. Your body, on the other hand, draws from a number of different energy sources, such as carbohydrate, fat, and protein. To a certain extent, the source of fuel your body uses is dictated by its availability. In other words, your body tends to use whatever you feed it. Consequently, when acetate levels rise, your body simply burns more acetate and less fat.

In essence, acetate pushes fat to the back of the queue. So here's what happens to fat metabolism after a drink or two:

1. A small portion of the alcohol is converted into fat.

2. Your liver then converts most of the alcohol into acetate.

3. The acetate is then released into your bloodstream and replaces fat as a source of fuel.

Your body's response to alcohol is very similar to the way it deals with excess carbohydrate. Although carbohydrate can be converted directly into fat, one of the main effects of overfeeding with carbohydrate is that it simply replaces fat as a source of energy. That's why any type of diet, whether it's high fat, high protein, or high carbohydrate, can lead to weight gain.

The bottom line is that even a small amount of alcohol (this study used two servings of vodka and lemonade) can have a big impact on the rate at which your body burns fat—even if the drink is low in calories.

---

* Siler, S. Q., R. A. Neese, and M. K. Hellerstein. "De Novo Lipogenesis, Lipid Kinetics, and Whole-Body Lipid Balances in Humans After Acute Alcohol Consumption." *American Journal of Clinical Nutrition* 70 (1999): 928–36.

RESEARCH UPDATE: Fat Burners and Free Radicals

One of the ways popular fat burners (such as Xenadrine and Hydroxycut) help you lose weight is to increase your metabolic rate. However, what's not so well known is that this increase in metabolic rate can also lead to a rise in the production of substances known as *free radicals*.

Free radicals are molecules with an unpaired electron. Although they've been implicated in many diseases, they are a normal part of your body chemistry and can help to keep you healthy. White blood cells, for example, use free radicals to attack viruses and bacteria.

Antioxidants

Optimal health requires a balance between free radical generation and antioxidant protection. One of the functions of an antioxidant is to "quench" free radicals before they create too much damage. Slice an apple in half and watch it turn brown: that's an example of free radical damage. Dip the apple in lemon juice and the rate at which it turns brown is slowed. That's because the antioxidant vitamin C in the lemon juice slows the rate of oxidative damage.

This is one of the reasons antioxidant vitamin supplements (such as vitamins A, C, and E) have become so popular. How-ever, while you can get *some* antioxidants from supplements, it's extremely difficult to get *all* the nutrients you need from a pill.

There are eight different compounds that make up vitamin E, for example, yet most vitamin supplements contain just one (usually alpha-tocopherol). Of course, this doesn't mean that vitamin pills are useless. Rather, they are a *supplement to*, not a *replacement for*, a nutrient-dense diet.

Relying on supplements alone also ignores the fact that there are many different nutrients in fruit and vegetables besides vitamins. And, contrary to popular belief, some of these nutrients become *more* available for absorption when the foods are cooked (as opposed to eating them raw). Antioxidant activity in cooked sweet yellow corn, for example, is 44 percent higher than in the same corn before cooking.

Cooking

While it's true that vitamin C is partially destroyed by cooking, the antioxidant activity of other nutrients in the food can be increased by cooking. In fact, only a very small amount of an apple's antioxidant activity comes from vitamin C. Instead, a combination of phytochemicals supplies the antioxidants in apples.

The term *phyto* comes from the Greek word meaning "plant." You'll see the terms *phytochemical* and *phytonutrient* used interchangeably—they both mean essentially the same thing.

Of all the phytonutrients, we probably know the most about carotenoids. They make tomatoes red, carrots orange, and corn yellow. The importance of carotenoids was first established back in 1919. Harry Steenbock, a biochemist at the University of Wisconsin, fed rats one of two diets. One diet contained a lot of "white" food, such as white corn, parsnips, and potatoes. The second diet was rich in "yellow" foods, such as yellow corn and carrots. The rats on the yellow diet thrived. Those on the white diet died within three months.

The work of Dr. Rui Hai Liu, assistant professor of food science at Cornell University, shows that heating certain foods increases the availability of some phytonutrients. This is in contrast to the conventional wisdom suggesting that cooking vegetables reduces their nutritional value. In his earlier research, Liu found that cooking tomatoes triggers a rise in total antioxidant activity, mainly due to an increase in lycopene—a phytochemical that makes tomatoes red.*

Of course, these findings don't necessarily apply to all nutrients in all foods. However, including more vegetables in your diet—whether they're raw or cooked—is an important step for anyone who wants to build a healthier body.

---

* Dewanto, V., X. Wu, and R. H. Liu. "Processed Sweet Corn Has Higher Antioxidant Activity." *Journal of Agricultural and Food Chemistry* 50 (2002): 4959–64.

---

fat. They also have a lot more muscle than their lean counterparts; it's just well hidden.

Dr. Forbes has discovered that the amount of fat and muscle you gain when you overfeed depends on how much body fat you have to start with. When he reviewed a number of studies where test subjects were overfed for a minimum of three weeks, he discov-ered that for every 10 pounds of weight gained by an *overweight* individual, 4 pounds came from lean tissue and 6 pounds from fat. For every 10 pounds of weight gained by a *lean* individual, 7 pounds came from lean tissue and 3 pounds from fat.

Of course, more *lean* tissue doesn't necessarily equate to more *muscle* tissue. Stored fluid and carbohydrate also contribute to gains in lean tissue.

These figures shouldn't be taken as an accurate indication of what you should expect to gain when you overfeed. After all, everyone has a slightly different definition of what *lean* means. Moreover, the longer the period of overfeeding, the greater the chances that the weight you gain will be in the form of fat. Rather, these numbers illustrate the principle that it's best to focus all your efforts on losing fat *before* trying to build muscle.

It's also worth pointing out that a period of controlled overfeeding should be relatively short (no longer than eight weeks). If it lasts too long, your body fat levels will rise, and the proportion of fat weight you gain will increase. And don't try to add weight too quickly. If you're *consistently* gaining more than 1 pound of weight each week, the chances are that a lot of it is fat rather than muscle.

LOW-FAT DIETS

Researchers from Boston have shown that a diet containing more fat could make it easier for you to lose weight and keep it off longer. Although low-fat diets are often used by people wanting to lose weight, this latest study shows that a low-calorie diet containing a higher percentage of fat is a far better option.[2]

A total of 101 overweight men and women were split into two groups. The first group consumed a diet deriving 35 percent of its calories from fat. The second group consumed a low-fat diet with 20 percent of the total calories from fat. Eighteen months later, the average weight loss in the group consuming the moderate-fat diet was

9 pounds. In contrast, the group consuming the low-fat diet had actually put on over 6 pounds. Moreover, 8 out of 10 subjects on the low-fat diet had quit after 18 months, compared to only 5 out of 10 on the moderate-fat diet.

One of the problems with low-fat diets is that they tend to restrict your choice of food. This could be the reason 8 out of 10 subjects had given up after 18 months. Moreover, foods commonly included in low-fat diets (such as meal replacement bars, ready-made low-fat meals, and low-fat desserts) contain ingredients with the potential to put the brakes on fat loss.

If you've ever tried to lose weight with a low-fat diet, chances are you felt hungry most of the time. That's because certain types of low-fat foods can trigger hormonal changes that stimulate your appetite. This promotes excessive food intake in people who are overweight.

Dietary fat has been demonized over the past two decades. However, this study shows that a low-calorie diet deriving 35 percent of its total calories from fat will help you lose weight and keep it off longer. It adds to the growing body of evidence showing that the various forms of dietary fat—polyunsaturated, monounsaturated, and saturated—all have an important role to play in a healthy diet.

WHEN TO CHEAT ON YOUR DIET

If you've been dieting for some time, chances are you've developed the odd craving or two for a few of the foods on your "banned" list. Now researchers from the Washington University School of Medicine have shown that the calories in a "cheat" meal may be

2 McManus, K., L. Antinoro, and F. Sacks. "A Randomized Controlled Trial of a Moderate-Fat, Low-Energy Diet Compared with a Low-Fat, Low-Energy Diet for Weight Loss in Overweight Adults." *International Journal of Obesity and Related Metabolic Disorders* 25 (2001): 1503–11.

RESEARCH UPDATE: Cholesterol

A diet that is high in saturated fat is supposed to lead to a rise in a person's cholesterol levels. This, in turn, is thought to increase the risk of heart disease. However, while some studies do show a link between saturated fat and heart disease, many others do not. The problem is, we usually hear only about the studies that do!

Many people don't realize that low cholesterol levels aren't necessarily healthy. For instance, men and women with low cholesterol are more likely to suffer from anxiety and depression. More interesting still, your cholesterol levels can rise even if you lose weight using a combination of diet and exercise.

Some evidence of this comes from researchers at the United States Army Research Institute of Environmental Medicine.* They tracked two groups of men taking part in a U.S. Army Ranger course lasting eight weeks. The course was divided into four phases. Each phase lasted two weeks and took place in four different environments:

- A temperate forest at Fort Benning, Georgia
- The Chihuahuan Desert near El Paso, Texas
- The Blue Ridge Mountains in northern Georgia
- A coastal swamp in Florida

Not only were the soldiers consuming an extremely low-calorie diet (one meal per day in some cases, leading to overwhelming hunger and fatigue), they were also subjected to other sources of both physical and mental stress:

- Typically, they slept for fewer than four hours each night.
- They were exposed to extremes of hot and cold weather, with relative humidity reaching an average of 92 percent during the swamp phase of training.
- Each day involved patrols in hostile terrain with loaded rucksacks weighing over 70 pounds.

As you can imagine, both groups of soldiers lost a lot of weight. In fact, the average weight loss in one group was 26 pounds, 16 pounds of which came from fat.

The other 10 pounds were lost from sources other than fat (such as lean muscle).

Despite the fact that the soldiers lost weight, exercised regularly, and consumed a low-calorie diet, their total cholesterol levels went up. Cholesterol levels dropped during the first two weeks of the study, then rose for the remainder of the trial. In fact, average cholesterol levels rose from 158 to 217 mg/dl (milligrams per deciliter). One important factor to notice in this study is the massive loss of lean muscle tissue in both groups of soldiers.

Although it can be tempting to speed up weight loss by restricting your calorie intake excessively, there's a good chance that much of the weight you lose will come from muscle, not fat. This has the effect of slowing your metabolic rate, making further weight loss more difficult.

The bottom line is that diet and exercise aren't the only things affecting how much cholesterol is in your blood. Both physical and mental stress (and probably many other factors we don't know about yet) seem to play an important role in determining your cholesterol levels.

* Friedl, K. E., R. J. Moore, R. W. Hoyt, L. J. Marchitelli, L. E. Martinez-Lopez, and E. W. Askew. "Endocrine Markers of Semistarvation in Healthy Lean Men in a Multistressor Environment." *Journal of Applied Physiology* 88 (2000): 1820–30.

less likely to get stored as fat if you eat them after exercise.[3]

The study showed that just one 60-minute workout could help to "divert" fat and sugar into muscle, rather than fat tissue. This should come as good news for anyone who's been dieting for some time and wants to indulge without feeling guilty.

Specifically, the research team found that exercise increases the activity of two enzymes—GLUT-4 and lipoprotein lipase. These enzymes are responsible for transporting glucose and fat into your muscles.

Lipoprotein lipase (LPL) plays an important role in both the storage and oxidation of body fat. When fat is

3 Greiwe, J. S., J. O. Holloszy, and C. F. Semenkovich. "Exercise Induces Lipoprotein Lipase and GLUT-4 Protein in Muscle Independent of Adrenergic-Receptor Signaling." *Journal of Applied Physiology* 89 (2000): 176–81.

RESEARCH UPDATE: CitriMax

Researchers from the Netherlands report that the popular dietary supplement Citri-Max (also known as hydroxycitric acid, HCA, or Garcinia cambogia) has no effect on the amount of fat you burn during exercise.* An ingredient found in many weight loss supplements, HCA is found in the rind of the fruit of Garcinia cambogia, which is used in Asian cuisine. HCA is certainly nothing new. Animal studies as far back as the 1970s show that large doses of HCA inhibit the conversion of carbohydrate to fat.

HCA and Fat Loss

More recently, it has been claimed that HCA can reduce cell levels of malonyl-CoA (an enzyme that slows the rate at which fat is burned as energy). In theory, at least, this would increase the number of fat calories you burn during exercise, speeding up weight loss.

Putting the theory to the test, a team of scientists from Maastricht University arranged for a group of 10 cyclists to take part in two trials. Both tests involved two hours of cycling. During the first trial, the cyclists consumed a drink containing 18 grams of HCA. In trial two, they were given plain water. When they used HCA, the cyclists burned an average of 0.68 grams of fat per minute of exercise. When they weren't given HCA, the cyclists burned an average of 0.66 grams of fat per minute of exercise.

Not much difference, right? Now, despite the fact that HCA before and during exercise has little effect on the amount of fat you burn, what's interesting is the large drop in lactic acid levels seen in subjects using HCA. After 30 minutes of exercise, lactic acid levels were significantly lower in subjects using HCA. And for the rest of the two-hour ride, lactic acid levels remained lower in the cyclists using HCA.

Why Lactic Acid Isn't a Waste Product

Lactic acid contributes to that burning sensation you get in your muscles when you exercise. Even at rest, your body produces some lactic acid. During exercise, however, lactic acid can build up because the rate of production is greater than the rate of removal.

Although it's often thought of as a waste product, lactic acid can actually be recycled by your liver and used as energy. Potentially, HCA could increase the rate at which your liver converts lactic acid into glucose. However, whether this would actually improve your performance in the gym is open to debate.

The amount of HCA used in this study was extremely high (6 to 30 times the amount used in previous studies), and most people don't have the time to sit on a bike for two hours. What is clear from this research is that using HCA before and during exercise won't affect the number of fat calories you burn for energy.

* Van Loon, L. J., J. J. van Rooijen, B. Niesen, H. Verhagen, W. H. Saris, and A. J. Wagenmakers. "Effects of Acute (-)-Hydroxycitrate Supplementation on Substrate Metabolism at Rest and During Exercise in Humans." *American Journal of Clinical Nutrition* 72 (2000): 1445–50.

oxidized, it is burned for energy. If you oxidize more fat than you store, eventually you'll lose weight.

Whether LPL promotes fat storage or fat oxidation depends on whether it's expressed in muscle or fat. LPL in fat tissue takes fat from the blood and stores it as body fat. LPL in muscle tissue diverts fat away from storage in fat tissue and toward oxidation.

Animal studies show that mice with high levels of LPL in their muscles are resistant to the effects of a high-fat diet. Some scientists think drugs that increase LPL in muscle could represent one way to tackle the growing problem of obesity. Of course, this doesn't mean that exercise gives you the freedom to eat all you want.

The key to losing weight is to burn more calories than you take in from your diet. If you simply replace the extra energy you've expended during exercise with additional calories from your diet, your weight won't change. And more than one or two "cheat" meals each week can easily put the brakes on weight loss. However, the bottom line is that the calories in a cheat meal are less likely to be stored as fat if you eat them a few hours after you exercise.

HOW TO PREVENT REGAINING WEIGHT

A new study has shown why it's so difficult to prevent regaining weight after several months of dieting. A research team based at Maastricht University showed that just 10 weeks on a very low-calorie diet actually reduces the number of fat calories your body burns each day.[4] This postdiet drop in fat oxidation could explain why many people find it such a challenge to prevent weight regain.

A group of 40 overweight men took part in the study. They were divided into two groups: diet only and diet plus aerobic exercise. During the first six weeks of the study, subjects in both groups were given a very low calorie diet, just 500 calories daily. From weeks 7 to 10, they gradually increased their food intake. The men in the exercise group completed three sessions per week consisting of walking and underwater exercise. Each workout lasted for around one hour. Here are the results for both groups following 10 to 12 weeks of diet and exercise:

Diet only	Diet plus exercise
Fat loss: 28 pounds	Fat loss: 28 pounds
Muscle loss: 5 pounds	Muscle loss: 6 pounds

As you can see, both groups lost roughly the same amount of fat and muscle. However, tests showed that the subjects who didn't exercise had a reduced capacity to burn fat, both at rest and during exercise. This postdiet decline in the number of fat calories used as energy offers one explanation as to why it's so easy to put weight back on after you've lost it. The good news is that exercise serves to completely block this decline, which could help you prevent weight regain.

There are two important points you can take from this study. Low-intensity aerobic exercise (such as walking) performed three times per week has little effect on the rate at which you lose fat. A combination of weight training and interval exercise is a far more effective way to train if you want to lose fat faster.

The benefits of low-intensity aerobic exercise are more apparent when you're trying to keep the weight off. The exercise doesn't have to be particularly vigorous or demanding. Just three hours of walking each week appears adequate to prevent the post-diet decline in fat oxidation.

NUTRITION INFORMATION

The majority of nutrition information you read is based on the amount of food you eat. That is, when you eat more calories than you burn, you'll gain weight. Eat fewer calories than you burn, and you'll lose weight.

While this nutrition information is true to a certain extent, it tends to promote the idea that food is only a source of fuel—a way of providing your body with energy. In truth, what you eat is far more important than that.

In fact, the food you eat *today* is what you become *tomorrow*. Think about it—old skin, muscle, and brain cells are constantly replaced with new ones. And the material your body uses to accomplish this incredible feat of construction is the food you eat.

Some evidence for this comes from a trial published in the *American*

4 Van Aggel-Leijssen, D. P. C., W. H. M. Saris, G. B. Hul, and M. A. van Baak. "Short-Term Effects of Weight Loss With or Without Low-Intensity Exercise Training on Fat Metabolism in Obese Men." *American Journal of Clinical Nutrition* 73 (2001): 523–31.

RESEARCH UPDATE:
The Fidget Factor

Some people seem to be able to eat whatever they want and not gain weight. The reason, say researchers from Mayo Clinic, is that they burn hundreds of extra calories in the activities of daily living when they overeat. Mayo Clinic researchers had 16 people overeat for two months and tracked what happened to the food the participants consumed, in terms of whether it was burned off as energy or stored as fat.*

They found that the key factor in predicting fat gain was the change in calories burned during the normal activities of daily living—such as fidgeting, moving around, or changing posture. They labeled this factor NEAT (non-exercise activity thermogenesis). "Those people who had the greatest increase in NEAT gained the least fat, and those who had the least change gained the most," says James Levine, M.D., a Mayo Clinic endocrinolo-

gist. Dr. Levine, Michael Jensen, M.D., and Norman Eberhardt, Ph.D., of Mayo Clinic's Endocrine Research Unit, were the authors of the report. "When people overeat, NEAT switches on in some people to 'waste' this excess energy," says Dr. Jensen. Conversely, the failure to switch this on allows the calories to be stored as fat.

This study suggests that efforts to activate NEAT, perhaps through behavioral cues, may help prevent obesity. Fat gain occurs when you take in more calories than you burn. The three main factors involved in the burning of calories are as follows:

1. Basal metabolic rate (BMR)—burning of energy when your body is at rest

2. Postprandial thermogenesis—energy burned in the digestion, absorption, and storage of food in your body

3. Physical activity—exercise (sports and fitness activities) and NEAT

The researchers measured the contributions of each of these factors in the participants' total daily energy expenditure. For the first two weeks of the study, participants were fed so as to establish the dietary intake necessary to maintain a stable body weight. For the next eight weeks, they were fed an additional 1,000 calories (equivalent to two Big Macs) daily. Participants were limited to low levels of exercise, which was monitored.

NEAT Reduces Fat Gain
Using sophisticated techniques, the researchers were able to precisely measure the fate of the additional 1,000 calories in each subject. The 16 volunteers gained an average of 10 pounds in the two months of the study. However, weight gain varied from 2 pounds to almost 16 pounds. Those with the greatest increase in NEAT (the most was 692 calories per day) gained the least amount of fat.

* Levine, J. A., N. L. Eberhardt, and M. D. Jensen. "Role of Non-Exercise Activity Thermogenesis in Resistance to Fat Gain in Humans." *Science* 8 (1999): 212–14.

Journal of Clinical Nutrition.[5] A group of healthy adults (25 men and 7 women) was split into two groups and assigned to one of two diets for a period of three months. The first group was fed a diet high in saturated fat, while the second group consumed a diet high in monounsaturated fat. Some of the subjects in each group also received fish oil capsules (containing just under 4 grams of omega-3 fatty acids).

At the end of the study, all of the study participants volunteered to have

a small part of the muscle tissue in their thighs taken out and examined by the researchers. The results showed that the type of fat found in muscle cells was *directly related* to the type of fat in the diet. For instance, the proportion of omega-3 fatty acids in muscle phospholipids was almost three times higher in subjects given fish oil compared to those given a placebo.

What all of this means is that when planning your diet, it's important to consider not only the *quantity* of the food you eat but the *quality* of

5 Andersson, A., C. Nalsen, S. Tengblad, and B. Vessby. "Fatty Acid Composition of Skeletal Muscle Reflects Dietary Fat Composition in Humans." *American Journal of Clinical Nutrition* 76 (2002): 1222–29.

the ingredients as well. For example, even though they might be low in calories, many ready-made meals are loaded with preservatives, hydrogenated oils, and low-quality protein.

The food you eat is more than just fuel. It provides the building blocks for the body you live in every day. It affects the way you think and feel—not just today, but in the coming weeks, months, and years. You really *are* what you eat!

PART II

New Strategies
for Exercise

4

Focusing on Realistic Results

One thing I've learned from all the letters I've received is that people don't have as much time to exercise as they'd like. Many still believe it takes long hours in the gym and lots of exercises to get great results. Some people wish they could train three hours! And if they can't work out for as long as they believe they should or do all the exercises they want, they think they're not getting any results. But could it be that *because* they work out so long and so often, they are not getting results?

I think so. Too many exercises and too much time in the gym are definitely not to your advantage when it comes to effective progressive resistance training.

Ever stop for a moment and look at the covers of diet, health, and fitness magazines and books? I'm holding one right now that promises you will "Lose Weight Fast." Here's another one that encourages you to "Eat Anything You Want." Still another promises "The No-Exercise Way to a Great Body."

We've seen these hyped-up headlines and promises so often and from so many places that we are not even affected by them anymore. These promises are not just unrealistic but confusing, because they don't accurately tell you what's *really* needed to get you from where you are to where you want to be.

It's time to readjust your thinking about what it's going to take for you to achieve your body goals. In all the years I've been training and observing what a normal, non–chemically enhanced bodybuilder can achieve, here's what I've found.

REALISTIC RESULTS

Lots of bodybuilders want a great-looking chest, a V-taper back, broad shoulders, and a flat stomach with visible abs. Almost every bodybuilder I've talked to wants to have bigger and stronger arms.

For any bodypart, the size and shape potential of your muscles lies in your genes. I've seen people with great genes do very little—in the way of amount of weights used, exercises done, or time spent working out—and they grow like weeds with bodyparts that are amazing. These people are the exception and definitely not the rule when it comes to training.

I've seen far more who really bust their butts in the gym. They do the right workouts, eat the right things, get enough rest, and stay with it year after year. And they make excellent gains, but not as quickly or with such impressive results as the genetic wonders.

Here's an experiment for you. Next time you're in the gym, take a good look at other people's physiques. Observe how their bodyparts are put together. You're going to see some interesting things. Some people will have big, round, full muscles, and others will not. Some people will have low, wide, diamond-shaped calves, and others will have high calves that resemble a baseball stuck inside a garden hose.

Yes, even though we all have two arms, two legs, one back, one chest, and two shoulders, these bodyparts will all look different. And that's OK. One look is not necessarily better than another (unless you're in a physique contest); it's just the unique way that each of us was blessed and put together genetically.

So is there anything you can do about it? Well, you're not going to change your genetics, so you can forget about that. You *can* take the body you have and make it your best, but you need to accept certain limitations:

- Some of your bodyparts will grow and get stronger much faster than others.
- Some bodyparts will not significantly respond or radically change their size and shape regardless of how much weight you use, how many workouts you do, or how many years you train. Many would

like you to believe otherwise, but in the 25-plus years I've been working out, I've seen this proven over and over again.

- If you're looking to build bigger arms, know that on average—unless you're one of those genetically blessed—*you will need to put on about 10 pounds of bodyweight for every one inch you put on your arms.*
- You'll never reach your bodybuilding size and strength potential unless you train legs hard and heavy. Squats will do more to pack size and strength on your body than any other exercise you can do. Deadlifts are excellent, but squats are still the king.

For Those Who Have Trained 1 to 24 Months

You can expect to see your body changing shape, size, strength, and condition faster than in any other period. I gained 30 pounds in my first year of working out and 35 pounds in my second year for a total of 65 pounds, and I have never used any drugs.

For Those Who Have Trained 25 to 60 Months

You will notice the rate and speed of your gains gradually tapering down. Expect strength to increase, but muscle size gains (the kind you will be able to keep) to be in the 2- to 5-pound-per-year range.

For Those Who Have Trained More than Five Years

You will notice two distinct things:

1. You will have reached (or will be close to reaching) the limit of the normal muscular size that your body can build, adapt, and carry. Remember, I'm talking about doing all this stuff naturally here, so when you throw drugs into the

mix, it changes *everything* . . . but for only a short time.

2. While the increases in strength will have slowed down, you will still be able to get stronger, provided that you train right and give your body plenty of rest. As the body's ability to generate the intensity to gain strength *increases*, its capacity to recover from those hard workouts *decreases*. In other words, you just need to take more time off if you're hitting the iron hard.

Many people don't want to do that, though, as evidenced by the following story. Let's call my friend Kevin. He's 5'10" and weighs 180, and he trains like there's no tomorrow. For months he was in the gym, training more than two hours a workout, doing set after set with heavy weights.

His gains in muscle size and strength were amazing. His body was transforming—he went from being a skinny guy to having a V-taper and muscle. All this newfound strength and size was pretty addicting to Kevin. He was getting attention he never had and was digging it. But then things changed.

In a matter of only a few months of this kind of "pound the crap out of the body" training insanity, he began to sleep less at night and found himself getting irritable. His strength started to taper off, reached the point where he wasn't getting any stronger, and then began decreasing.

So he started training harder, thinking that he was doing something wrong and not working out hard enough for his body to continue growing and getting stronger like he had experienced.

Then one day he felt a twinge in his shoulder. Nothing major, mind you, but a little pain nonetheless. He thought he could work through it,

but after a few workouts he realized that he needed to back *way* off from doing any exercises that made that area hurt.

However, he didn't want to do that because he believed that if he wasn't hitting hard, he wasn't doing what it takes to get bigger and stronger. And if he wasn't getting the results he needed (he didn't just *want* them now . . . he was addicted to them and he *needed* them), he would be angry with himself, with those around him, and with the world.

Luckily, Kevin woke up and will make a full recovery. Many others never stop the training habits that hurt them. Joe Weider once told me, "The only way many of these folks will cut back or stop training in wrong ways is if they get injured, and it's the injury that *makes* them stop."

Friend, you don't need heavy weights to get great results. One of the best dual-benefit training methods (offering both aerobic and strength benefits) is so simple, even for an advanced bodybuilder: it's 6 sets of 12. Six sets per bodypart of 12 reps per set with only 20 seconds of rest between sets.

Think of it: you can do 6 sets of 6 reps with 100 pounds on the dumbbell incline press for chest—with much more rest needed between sets and higher risk of injury—for a total of 3,600 total pounds lifted. Or you can do 6 sets of 12 reps with 70 pounds for a total of 5,040 pounds lifted, and with a much lower risk of injury and a far greater aerobic benefit. You'll be amazed at how "heavy" those 70-pound dumbbells feel after your fifth set of 12 reps with them.

Graduating from *Bodybuilding 101* to *Bodybuilding 201* should have made you a smarter trainer. If not, put this book down and go back and reread *101*. It's pointless to go forward unless you've stopped doing the things that are hurting you and are ready for the things that won't.

Let me share with you some of the things I've found that can really help take it to the next level.

WORKOUT ROUTINES

Researchers have long argued that workout routines without any form of aerobic exercise offer little in the way of health benefits, claiming your heart and lungs don't get the kind of workout they would from activities such as brisk walking or running.

However, Harvard scientists have shown that men who include weight training in their workout routines for just 30 minutes each week reduce their risk of heart disease by 23 percent compared to those not training with weights. The study—published in the *Journal of the American Medical Association*—is based on medical records and questionnaires given to 44,452 male dentists, optometrists, pharmacists, podiatrists, osteopaths, and veterinarians enrolled in the Health Professionals Follow-Up Study.[1] Participants were interviewed every two years between 1986 and the beginning of 1998.

The association between aerobic workout routines and a reduced risk of heart disease was expected. Men who ran for one hour or more each week reduced their risk by 42 percent compared to nonrunners. Walking at a brisk pace for more than 30 minutes was linked to an 18 percent reduction compared to the men who didn't walk.

Weight Training
More surprising were the results showing a similar risk reduction with weight training. In contrast, cycling and swimming did not appear to protect against heart disease. The authors attributed this finding to the intensity at which study participants performed these activities. Had they been done at a higher intensity, they likely would also have been linked with lower rates of disease.

"More intense aerobic exercise is more effective in improving cardiovascular fitness because it requires the heart muscle to work harder, to pump more blood, to get more oxygen," says Dr. Frank Hu. Hu is the senior author of the study and an associate professor of nutrition at Harvard School of Public Health. "If the exercise is suitable for the person, I think people should aim for more rigorous exercise given the amount of energy expenditure."

In other words, if two people spend the same amount of time exercising, the person doing the more intense exercise will benefit more. It's possible that the health benefits of exercise are linked simply to the number of calories you burn. This means that if you're pushed for time, you can burn 500 calories by doing some kind of intense exercise (such as weight training) for half an hour, rather than walking at a low intensity for 45 minutes or longer.

The health benefits from weight training might result in part from a drop in blood pressure and body fat. Weight training is very useful in improving insulin sensitivity, reducing fat mass, and preserving lean muscle. Over time, it appears these effects translate into less cardiovascular disease in the long run.

Of course, this doesn't mean that your workout routines shouldn't

---

1 M. Tanasescu, M. F. Leitzmann, E. B. Rimm, W. C. Willett, M. J. Stampfer, and F. B. Hu. "Exercise Type and Intensity in Relation to Coronary Heart Disease in Men." *Journal of the American Medical Association* 288 (2002): 1994–2000.

RESEARCH UPDATE: Fit or Fat?

New research has shown that being fit can counter some of the health risks linked to excess body fat. Most researchers agree that too much fat increases your risk of coronary heart disease. In contrast, a lower level of fat is supposed to reduce the risk. However, a recent trial by researchers from the Cooper Institute in Dallas and the University of Houston showed that lean men had increased longevity only if they were physically fit. Moreover, obese men who were fit were less likely to die from cardiovascular disease than lean men who were unfit.*

The research team tracked a group of 21,925 men who had complete medical evaluations between 1971 and 1989. The men were split into three different groups based on their body fat levels, as follows:

- Lean (less than 16.7 percent body fat)
- Normal (between 16.7 and 25 percent body fat)
- Obese (above 25 percent body fat)

Fitness levels were tested using a treadmill endurance test. The men in the least-fit 20 percent of each age group were classified as physically unfit. The rest were classified as being fit. During an average follow-up period of eight years, the results showed that aerobic fitness served to protect against some of the health risks associated with excess body fat.

Not surprisingly, those with the highest risk of heart disease were obese and unfit. The following list shows the relative risk of death from cardiovascular disease in the different groups of men. Unfit men with a normal level of body fat, for example, have a relative risk of 3.0. In simple terms, this means they are three times more likely to die from cardiovascular disease than lean, fit men (who have a relative risk of 1.0).

- Fit and lean: 1.0
- Fit and obese: 1.0
- Fit and normal: 1.4
- Unfit and normal: 1.4
- Unfit and lean: 3.0
- Unfit and obese: 3.2

All subjects in this study were white men, so the findings don't necessarily apply to all populations. However, the results do show that fit men are likely to live longer than unfit men, regardless of body composition.

Now, this isn't an endorsement for being overweight. After all, those with the highest risk of heart disease were obese and unfit. But it does show that regular physical activity is beneficial even if it doesn't lead to weight loss.

---

* Lee, D. D., S. N. Blair, and A. S. Jackson. "Cardiorespiratory Fitness, Body Composition, and All-Cause and Cardiovascular Disease Mortality in Men." *American Journal of Clinical Nutrition* 69 (1999): 373–80.

include aerobic exercise—just that they don't have to.

OVERTRAINING

The whole point of training is to improve in some way. This means you must apply the principle of *progressive overload*—to continually demand more of your body in an attempt to make it leaner, fitter, stronger, or healthier. Too much training, however, especially when it's combined with a low-calorie diet, can lead to a condition known as *overtraining*.

You know you're overtraining when you're training excessively, but your performance in the gym is consistently getting worse. This drop in performance is usually accompanied by changes in mood as well as a number of biochemical and physiological symptoms. Joint and muscle pain, fatigue, and loss of appetite are just a few signs of overtraining.

Overtraining can best be defined as the state where rest is no longer adequate to allow for recovery. *Overtraining syndrome* is the name given to the collection of emotional, behavioral, and physical symptoms that persist for weeks (maybe even months).

Overtraining often stems from the frustration many people feel at their slow rate of progress—especially if they've been training for some time.

This leads them to spend longer and longer in the gym in the belief that if a little exercise is good, then more is better.

Overreaching describes a temporary decline in performance. Some athletes incorporate overreaching in their training cycle, but make sure to include the correct amount of recovery. Without this balance, overreaching can lead to overtraining.

Researchers have tried to determine what happens to athletes when they begin to overtrain. Although numerous measurements have been tested in an effort to spot overtraining in its early stages, none has proven totally effective. However, writing in the journal *Medicine and Science in Sports and Exercise*, Dr. Lucille Lakier Smith suggests that one common factor could be at the heart of many of the symptoms of overtraining.[2]

Cytokines

Most types of training lead to some form of injury known as a microtrauma—or, more accurately, adaptive microtrauma. The reason it's called adaptive is that the microtrauma leads to some kind of adaptation in bone, muscle, or connective tissue. That's why muscles get bigger and bones get stronger.

This small level of microtrauma leads to the production of substances called *cytokines* (pronounced si-to-kines). Cytokines are a little like hormones, and they can give you an early warning that you're about to enter an overtrained state. You see, your brain contains specific cytokine receptors. Think of cytokines as being like a key and receptors like a lock.

When cytokines bind these receptors, they lead to changes in mood. In fact, there is evidence to link cytokines with depression. Test subjects administered cytokines tend to become distressed. And the higher the level of cytokines, the worse the symptoms get.

Mood

Although a reduction in performance is normally considered a sign of overtraining, it can be preceded by changes in mood. If you're aware of this, you can prevent an overtrained state before it manifests itself as a decline in performance.

Dr. Michael Stone suggests that overtraining syndrome for someone following an anaerobic training program (such as strength training) manifests itself as anxiety or agitation. Aerobic exercise, on the other hand, can lead to feelings of depression.

Of course, overtraining isn't the only reason that you could be feeling anxious or depressed. However, if you are feeling a little down and you can't identify the cause, take a critical look at your exercise program. Although it's not always easy to do, taking one step back is sometimes what you need to do in order to take two steps forward.

2 Smith, L. L. "Cytokine Hypothesis of Overtraining: A Physiological Adaptation to Excessive Stress?" *Medicine and Science in Sports and Exercise* 32 (2000): 317–31.

5

Using a Training Log

Keeping a training log—a detailed record of your workout routines—is a great way to help you get past sticking points. A log will enable you to formulate new and varied routines so that you can enjoy great training success for many years.

It's simple, really—just keep a record of every workout you do. This practice is important for a number of reasons:

1. A log gives you a good indication of your training progress. If you're getting stronger, your body will show it.
2. A training log gives you precise information as to which exercises are working and which aren't. This valuable feedback allows you to keep the exercises that work for *your* body and eliminate the ones that don't.
3. You can refer to your training log at any time and formulate new routines from the set, rep, and weight combinations that *work best for you.*

For years, the best bodybuilders in the world have used training logs. Think about it: can you remember a workout you did four months ago that got your legs incredibly sore? You could if you looked it up in your training log.

I've always used a spiral-bound notebook, although there are logbooks on the market. There are five things you should include about each workout:

1. Date of workout
2. Bodypart worked
3. Exercises with sets, reps, and weights used
4. Workout notes immediately after the workout. This is where you can write down anything noteworthy about the workout, such as a great new exercise you tried or extra weight or reps you used.
5. Postworkout report, the following day. Here you should note which bodyparts were sore, which weren't, and the degree of soreness and how long it lasted.

Of course, you should feel free to keep track of any other information you find helpful, including what you ate just before your workout, how much water you drank, whether you had a good night's sleep, and so forth.

As you will see, keeping a workout logbook will focus your training big time. However, there may be workouts when your strength has plateaued or even decreased. But loss of strength does not necessarily mean a loss of muscle.

STRENGTH LOSS VERSUS MUSCLE LOSS

When they lose strength, most people automatically assume they've lost muscle. However, a new study has shown this isn't necessarily the case. Researchers from the College of William and Mary examined the effects of 14 days of inactivity on the strength and size of several muscles in the thigh. Although there was a drop in muscle strength, there was no evidence of any reduction in muscle size. Instead, the decline in strength was attributed to changes to the nervous system.[1]

Inside your body are billions of nerve cells. Give or take a factor of 10, there are probably the same number of nerve cells in your body as there are stars in our galaxy! The task of each nerve cell is to receive a message, then pass it on to other cells. Eventually the signal reaches the muscle.

The nerve and the muscle fibers it activates are called a motor unit. When a motor unit is called on, all of the muscle fibers in that motor unit contract. There is no such thing as a partial contraction of a motor unit—it either contracts or it doesn't. Instead, when you need to lift a heavy weight, your body simply recruits more motor units.

Neural Factors

In the early 1970s, researchers showed that 100 days of exercise led to a 90 percent increase in muscle strength. However, there was only a 25 percent increase in muscle size. In other words, you can get stronger without getting bigger.

Untrained individuals aren't able to use all the motor units available in a given muscle. However, when you start a training program, your ability to recruit motor units increases. As the program continues, an increase in muscle tissue makes a greater contribution to changes in strength. That's why someone with 20 years of training experience won't gain strength as fast as a beginner.

While the gains in strength at the start of a training program are due to neural factors, it also appears that the early drop in strength when you stop training is also related to changes to the nervous system.

The bottom line is that if you've missed training for a week or two, don't worry too much about losing muscle tissue. Any reduction in muscle strength is probably attributable to neural factors rather than to any muscle loss.

---

1 Deschenes, M. R., J. A. Giles, R. W. McCoy, J. S. Volek, A. L. Gomez, and W. J. Kraemer. "Neural Factors Account for Strength Decrements Observed After Short-Term Muscle Unloading." *American Journal of Physiology* 282 (2002): R578–R583.

6

The Weider Intensity Principles

If you're looking for great results from your weight training workouts, *intensity* is the name of the game. Remember: it's not how long you work out; it's what you do and how you do it *when* you work out that make all the difference. You need to find different ways of exercising that will increase the intensity of your workouts, and one of the best ways to do that is to use Weider intensity principles.

Many years ago, Joe Weider observed that many who trained with weights were making good progress following tried-and-true ways of lifting, but a handful of them were getting great results when they combined different ways of lifting. Joe carefully studied what these people were doing, then gave these methods names and refined them so that anyone using them in the specific ways he outlined could get great results. What Joe Weider did revolutionized the way people work out.

Once you start using the Weider intensity principles, you too can expect much better results from any workout you do. The following are my

favorite Weider intensity principles for the *Bodybuilding 201* athlete.

- **Superset.** Group two exercises together for opposing muscle groups, such as biceps curls and triceps pressdowns. As soon as you finish the set of biceps curls, immediately do a set of triceps pressdowns.
- **Tri-set.** Do three exercises for the same muscle group without a pause. Hitting the muscle from three angles makes this more of a shaping movement, but it will give you a great pump.
- **Giant set.** Do a series of four to six exercises for one muscle group, with little or no rest in between.
- **Descending set.** This is like stripping, or reducing, the weights within the set of an exercise, except with descending you take the weight off between each set. It's especially helpful if you have a partner to take the weight off for you (such as taking some plates off a barbell) so you can continue to train with very high intensity without stopping.

- **Pyramid.** This is the process of increasing the weight you use each set. For example, begin your first set with 60 percent of your one-rep max weight and increase the weight by 10 percent each succeeding set. You can also do the opposite: warm up for a few sets, use your heaviest weight for 6 to 8 reps, then decrease the weight by 10 percent each succeeding set.
- **Compound set.** Perform two back-to-back exercises for the same bodypart with little or no rest—for example, barbell curls immediately followed by a set of seated dumbbell incline curls.
- **Forced reps.** Forced reps work well when you use them after you've completed as many reps as you can by yourself. When you can no longer perform reps on your own, have a spotter give you just a little help so you can do another rep or two. Use this technique sparingly.
- **Flushing.** You need to get blood into the muscle to produce growth. A terrific way to do that is to do multiple sets for each bodypart, which will in turn produce a good pump in the muscle you're working and give you feedback that the muscle is being "flushed" with blood.
- **Burns.** Doing 2 to 3 short partial reps at the end of your regular set forces more blood and lactic acid into the muscle, and this pump gives a burn that can help add to the size and vascularity of a muscle.
- **Partial reps.** Partial reps (that is, reps that are not full-range movements) are an excellent way to increase power and size. Use partial reps at any time in your training: at the beginning, midpoint, and finish positions. With partial reps, you can use much heavier weights, which can greatly strengthen muscle and connective tissue.

- **Pre-exhaustion.** First, work a muscle group to fatigue in its primary motion by using an isolation movement (like dumbbell concentration curls for biceps). Then immediately superset that exercise with a secondary motion using a basic exercise (like barbell curls). Another example of using this principle is pre-exhausting the quads by doing leg extensions first, followed by squats or leg presses.
- **Double-split.** With the double-split, you work out twice in one day, working a different bodypart in each workout. You could work one part of your body in the morning and the other in the evening. Doing so allows your body to recover more quickly and gives you more energy and intensity for each workout.
- **Triple-split.** This is similar to double-split training, except you have three brief workouts per day instead of one or two longer ones. Use this only after you've reached superb conditioning from using double-split training, and don't use it too much or too often. This is an excellent technique to use to break through a peak or plateau in your training.
- **Rest-pause.** To use rest-pause, pick an exercise and do as much weight as you can for 2 to 3 reps, then rest for 30 to 45 seconds; do another 2 to 3 reps, then rest again for another 40 to 60 seconds; do another 2 reps, then rest again for 60 to 90 seconds; finish with another 1 to 2 reps.
- **Speed training.** This technique works great when using heavy weights with strict, controlled form. The key is to slowly lower the weight and then, once you reach the bottom part of the movement, bring the weight back up to the starting position with as much speed and explosive power as possible. With each succeeding rep, as the weight

RESEARCH UPDATE:
How to Turn Back the Clock

According to researchers at UT South-western Medical Center, just six months of exercise can reverse the decline in physical fitness associated with aging.* Their findings are based on test results of five healthy men, ages 50 to 51, who were originally studied in 1966 and volunteered to participate in a 30-year follow-up that began in 1996.

The study provides novel findings regarding the effects of two endurance training programs separated by a 30-year period. The 1966 study, considered one of the pivotal studies in exercise science, evaluated the response to endurance exercise training after a 20-day period of bedrest.

According to Dr. Darren McGuire, assistant professor of internal medicine and lead author of the study, "twenty days of bed rest—which is the ultimate 'sedentary' state—in these subjects when they were 20 years old had a more profound negative impact on their cardiovascular fitness than did 30 years of aging."

Fitness Levels Restored

McGuire and his team also report that an endurance training program was able to reverse *all* of the loss of cardiovascular fitness that resulted from 30 years of aging. The five study volunteers completed a six-month endurance training program. Two participants took part in walking exercises, two jogged, and the fifth trained on a stationary bicycle. The endurance training was increased weekly. By the end of the study, the subjects were exercising four to five times weekly, with each workout lasting for roughly one hour.

Combat Aging

"This study clearly provides evidence that even an older person who has failed to maintain fitness over time can benefit from an exercise program," said coauthor Dr. Benjamin Levine, associate professor of internal medicine and director of the Institute for Exercise and Environmental Medi-cine. Levine continued, "Moreover, if you stop exercise you can lose what you have gained relatively quickly. Therefore, exercise must be a lifelong health habit—like brushing your teeth or taking a shower—that can and should be sustained throughout life."

The researchers also found that age plays a factor in the mechanisms involved in age-related decline in aerobic power. The investigators report that in middle-aged adults the mechanisms responsible for decline in cardiovascular capacity are directly related to peripheral oxygen extraction—that is, the body's ability to receive, take up, and use oxygen.

In the 1966 study, the 20-year-old volunteers improved their maximal ability to perform exercise by increasing the amount of blood that the heart could pump and by increasing the amount of oxygen that could be extracted. In the present study the volunteers were only able to increase the amount of oxygen the muscles extracted.

---

* McGuire, D. K., B. D. Levine, J. W. Williamson, P. G. Snell, C. G. Blomqvist, B. Saltin, and J. H. Mitchell. "A 30-Year Follow-Up of the Dallas Bedrest and Training Study: II. Effect of Age on Cardiovascular Adaptation to Exercise Training." *Circulation* 104 (2001): 1358–66.

---

becomes more difficult to lift, keep pushing harder with more explosive power.

- **Eclectic training.** This type of training combines isolation and mass movements in one exercise, set, rep, or workout (for example, doing the first 6 reps for biceps with a heavy barbell standing curl and then doing the last 4 to 6 reps with a seated cable concentration curl).

- **Holistic training.** Your muscle cells contain proteins and energy systems that respond differently to different levels of exercise. Muscle-fiber pro-teins get larger when they perform against high-resistance loads. The cell's aerobic systems (mitochondria) respond to high-endurance training. That's why it's important that your training include a variety of heavy weights/low reps and light weights/high reps in order to maximize your results.

- **Reverse gravity.** Think of this as what you do when you resist the downward force of gravity on the weight as you lower it. One way to do this is to slowly lower a heavy barbell to your chest, then have a spotter return the barbell to the starting position so you can lower it again. In that way the whole exercise is concentrated on resisting gravity. You'll find this to be quite an intense form of training that stimulates loads of muscle growth but also loads of muscle soreness. This kind of negative or reverse gravity training should be used sparingly—not every workout, or even every other workout.

- **Staggered sets.** Stagger your smaller and slower-developing bodyparts between sets for larger muscle groups. An example would be doing a set of wrist curls or concentration curls between sets of leg presses or squats. This will allow you to train the bigger muscle group (legs, in this example) with plenty of energy and power while also working the smaller muscle (in this case, either forearms or biceps).

- **Cycle training.** Many bodybuilders who train heavy all the time are at greater risk of injury than those who cycle their training. The body is not a machine and can't be continually pushed and pounded without periods of rest and cycled training. Three cycles you should be concerned with are as follows:
  - *Mass cycle*: Moderate to heavy weights; 6 to 10 reps for upper body and 8 to 20 reps for lower body; no more than 90 seconds of rest between sets
  - *Power cycle*: Heavy weights; 3 to 8 reps; up to 3 minutes of rest between sets
  - *Cut cycle*: Light to moderate weights; 12 to 25 reps; no more than 45 seconds of rest between sets

  Stay on each cycle for six to eight weeks and take one full week off from training before moving to the next cycle.

- **Continuous tension.** Many bodybuilders don't give much thought to proper form, and many of them train so fast that they'll swing the weights from start to finish just so they can finish their set. Yet this prevents making the muscles work harder and more effectively and increases the risk of injury. To use this principle, try training slower and more deliberately and focus on putting constant tension on the muscle you're training, which in turn will make it work harder and thereby raise the intensity of your workout.

- **Isotension.** Feeling a muscle work is the key to getting the most from any exercise. To help create this mind-to-muscle link, regularly practice isotension. Without using any weights, flex the muscle you've been working and hold it in the peak contracted position for 3 to 6 seconds. Do this three times at the end of the last set of every bodypart workout.

- **Muscle confusion.** Your body adapts very quickly to the physical demands you place on it. If you do the same routine in the same way over and over, your body will stop responding. That's why you must change your workouts, exercises, sets, reps, weights, rest periods, angles, and degrees of intensity every time you work out. By doing so, you will keep your body off-guard and you'll continue to grow and get stronger.

- **Peak contraction.** Peak contraction is simply keeping full tension on any muscle you're working when it is in the peak contracted position. A good example of this is when you flex your biceps and keep them flexed with as much peak contraction force as you can muster for at least 3 seconds.

RESEARCH UPDATE:
How to Increase Your
Strength in Seconds

A team of Italian scientists have shown that you can easily increase your muscle strength in just a few seconds—simply by clenching your jaw!* Investigating the link between jaw action and muscular performance, the researchers asked a group of men to hold a heavy dumbbell at the midpoint of an arm curl.

Several different jaw positions were tested to see what effect they would have on the amount of time the men could hold the weight:

- An open mouth, without dental contact
- A closed mouth, with only light dental contact
- A maximum voluntary clench

Results showed that the men were able to hold the weight for longer when the jaw was clenched. So next time you find yourself struggling near the end of a heavy set, try clenching your jaw—there's a good chance it might help you push out a few extra reps.

* Ferrario, V. F., C. Sforza, G. Serrao, N. Fragnito, and G. Grassi. "The Influence of Different Jaw Positions on the Endurance and Electromyographic Pattern of the Biceps Brachii Muscle in Young Adults with Different Occlusal Characteristics." *Journal of Oral Rehabilitation* 28 (2001): 732–39.

7

Training and Nutrition for the Endomorph

One of the questions most asked by bodybuilders is "How should I train?" But there really is no definitive answer. We all have different body types, goals, levels of experience, motivation, training time, and nutritional needs and habits, and those differences must be considered when determining what is the best training program for *you*.

Because what works best for one person may not work for another, I will present some practical training advice based on one particular aspect: body type. Although many of the exercises I discuss will work for any build, it's *how* you do them that can make all the difference with regard to your body type.

In this chapter, I'll discuss training for the endomorph—the kind of body that tends to be heavyset. In Chapters 8 and 9 I will tell you how to train if you're an ectomorph or a mesomorph.

WHAT'S YOUR BODY TYPE?

Of all the topics I've written about over the years, one that has struck a

nerve with people is training for one's body type and customizing one's workouts and lifestyle for it.

By now you know that working out makes you feel and look good. When you hit the weights regularly, your body changes for the better. You also know that the basic exercises will help you get on the road to fitness success. But soon you'll reach a point where knowing your body type and how it responds to training will take on new importance.

The three basic body types are the following:

- **Endomorph:** Characterized by soft musculature, short neck, round face, wide hips, and an inclination toward heavy fat storage
- **Ectomorph:** Characterized by long arms and legs; short upper torso; long, narrow feet and hands; narrow chest and shoulders; very little fat storage; and long, thin muscles
- **Mesomorph:** Characterized by a large chest, long torso, great strength, and solid musculature

Although individuals are usually a combination of all three types, each person leans toward being one of the three types. Knowing how these different body types respond to training and diet will help you reach your bodybuilding goals more quickly.

Understanding your body type and its specific training and nutritional demands for growth presents new challenges for you. These challenges require that you have a solid game plan to be successful in your training.

THE ENDOMORPH TRAINING PHILOSOPHY: EMPHASIS ON INTENSITY AND AEROBICS

Endomorphs typically have a higher-than-normal percentage of body fat. Weight gains come easily, while losing body fat is much more difficult. On the plus side, many endomorphs are blessed with a big and wide bone structure.

Often, the weight that endomorphs gain stays right where they don't want it—on the abs, waist, and buttocks. As endomorphs begin weight training and bodybuilding, they tend to gain size—much of it muscle—fairly quickly. However, it often remains hidden under layers of fat. Ironically, an endomorph can have a body that's hard as a rock, yet good definition is always just out of reach.

Many endomorphs, because of their advantageous bone size and ability to put on muscle quickly, train with heavy weights and low reps. Often this a mistake. An endomorph should train with moderate poundage, high intensity, minimal rest between sets, and more frequent workouts. The goal is to amp up the metabolism, make the muscle burn, and carve new cuts and definition.

Another *very* important training element is cardiovascular fitness. Far too many endomorphs do weight training and nothing else. That's another big mistake. Endomorphs

will never achieve the degree of leanness they desire unless they have a good diet and train the cardiovascular system at least three times per week. Excellent cardiovascular workout choices include brisk walking outdoors or on the treadmill, working out on the stairclimber, riding a stationary or regular bike, racket sports, and hiking.

Be sure to do your cardiovascular training in the *target heart rate zone*. To compute your target heart rate zone, subtract your age from 220 and multiply that number by 0.6 and 0.8. The numbers you get represent a range of heartbeats per minute; when you exercise, check your pulse periodically to make sure your beats per minute are in that range. After a 5-minute warm-up, exercise in your target zone for 15 to 20 minutes, then cool down for 3 to 5 minutes.

High Reps, High Sets

Building muscle mass is generally relatively easy if you're an endomorph; keeping your fat level low may be more of a challenge. Endomorphs typically respond well to high-set (12 to 15), high-rep (12 to 20) training that allows for only brief rest between sets. They should train no more than four or five days per week—a two-on, one-off program would be a good choice.

Aerobic training using stationary bikes, treadmills, stairclimbers, or other machines for at least 20 to 30 minutes per workout should be included in your program. Keeping your caloric intake of protein, carbs, and fats to restricted levels is important, but not at the expense of going below your daily nutritional requirements for muscle repair and growth.

The Workout: Tips for Success

As always, keep your workouts fun. That means changing your training program regularly—like every second or third workout. Then try the following:

- Take three to five exercises that work well for each bodypart and use those as your pool of exercises to choose from for each workout.
- Choose two to three different exercises for each bodypart from the pool of exercises each workout.
- Do one basic movement (for example, dumbbell incline press for chest) and one to two isolation movements (dumbbell flye, pec deck, or cable crossover).
- Rest between sets no longer than 60 seconds.
- Keep your reps in the 9-to-12 range for upper body and 12-to-25 range for legs and calves.
- Each workout, vary the rest times, reps, sets, and weight. Keep your body constantly off-guard.

RESEARCH UPDATE:
Muscle Growth

Many people are concerned that adding aerobic exercise to their training program will slow down muscle growth. However, new research shows that strength training and aerobic exercise performed concurrently for 10 weeks won't interfere with gains in muscle size and strength.*

To examine the effect of aerobic exercise and strength training performed concurrently on the rate of muscle growth, researchers assigned a group of 30 healthy but untrained male subjects to one of three groups:

- Group one performed high-intensity strength training three days a week. The program involved eight exercises, with 4 sets of 5 to 7 repetitions completed for each exercise. The first set served as a warm-up. Subsequent sets were taken to the point of muscular failure. Subjects rested for 60 to 90 seconds between sets.
- Group two completed three sessions of moderate-intensity aerobic exercise each week. Each workout lasted 50 minutes.
- Subjects in group three combined aerobic exercise and strength training. Both workouts were performed on the same day, with the order of strength and aerobic exercise rotated each training day.

Subjects rested for 10 to 20 minutes between workouts. Muscle strength and size were measured before and after the program. The researchers also measured the size of individual muscle fibers in the thighs. As you can see in the chart below, combining aerobic exercise and high-intensity strength training didn't impair muscle growth.

[Editor's note: Type I fibers are also called red, slow-twitch endurance fibers that are primarily aerobic in nature. They also contain less glycogen than Type II fibers. Type II fibers are also called fast-twitch fibers and are used for powerful, fast movements.]

Strength group
Quadriceps size + 12%
Type II fiber size + 24%

Endurance group
Quadriceps size + 3%
Type II fiber size + 4.5%

Combined group
Quadriceps size + 14%
Type II fiber size + 28%

Gains in muscle strength, however, were slightly lower in the combined group compared to the strength training group (7 percent and 12 percent, respectively).

These findings do suggest that aerobic exercise and strength training performed concurrently for 10 weeks won't interfere with muscle growth. However, there are several important points about this study that you need to consider.

First, although the test subjects were healthy, they were untrained. Beginners usually show some kind of gain in muscle size and/or strength no matter what type of program they follow. If you have several years of training under your belt and you're following a split routine that involves training with weights five to six days each week, there's a good chance that aerobic exercise will impair gains in strength and size.

Moreover, although aerobic exercise is usually added to a program in order to speed up fat loss, the majority of research shows that aerobic exercise as it's traditionally performed has very little effect on the rate at which you lose fat.

A properly designed weight training program, combined with interval exercise, is far more effective at promoting fat loss while also preventing the loss of lean muscle tissue that often occurs during a low-calorie diet.

---

* McCarthy, J. P., M. A. Pozniak, and J. C. Agre. "Neuromuscular Adaptations to Concurrent Strength and Endurance Training." *Medicine and Science in Sports and Exercise* 16 (2002): 152–56.

- Train abdominals at the beginning of your workout.
- Do no more than 8 sets per bodypart.
- Work out on a split-training system. For example, on Monday work chest and arms, Tuesday work legs, and Wednesday work back and shoulders.
- Thursday is a day off from weight training. Repeat the training schedule on Friday.

ONE LAST WORD

One of the most important training tips for the endomorph to keep in mind is training intensity. The endomorph must constantly keep training intensity high. Make the body work harder by working smarter using the guidelines given in this chapter. Keep the workouts fresh and exciting, and don't allow yourself to fall into a rut. Do something different each workout.

8

Training and Nutrition for the Ectomorph

Ectomorphs tend to be thin, lean, and lanky. Typically, an ectomorph will have a short upper torso; long arms and legs; narrow chest, shoulders, feet, and hands; and long, thin muscles.

Ectomorphs are leaders in the expedition for muscle size and weight. However difficult it may seem for ectomorphs to gain slabs of beef or become champion bodybuilders, they shouldn't lose hope. Champions like three-time Mr. Olympia Frank Zane and many other great bodybuilders were at one time ectomorphs.

THE IMPORTANCE OF INTENSITY

If you're an ectomorph, building muscle mass can be quite a challenge indeed. Putting on size may seem like it takes forever if you're not following a solid game plan. However, with proper guidelines, you can achieve your bodybuilding goals quickly. The following tips will help:

- Do the basic exercises that emphasize power movements for building mass. Exercises like squats, deadlifts, presses, chins, rows, and barbell curls are excellent mass builders.
- Keep your reps in the 6-to-8 range and sets in the 8-to-12 range. Be sure to give your body enough rest between sets so you can continue to lift heavy weight with good form in order to induce muscle-fiber stimulation for growth.
- Your training goal should be less volume and more intensity. Train no more than three days per week in order to give your body sufficient time for recuperation, repair, and growth. The Monday-Wednesday-Friday workout schedule is ideal.

Nutrition is a big factor in gaining weight and muscle mass for the ectomorph; it's important to take in extra calories throughout the day. Weight gain powders and protein drinks complement an overall solid nutritional plan while boosting caloric intake. Limit outside activities in order to save energy for building muscle mass.

Here are some other training and nutrition tips that are sure to help ectomorphs in muscle-building and strength-gaining goals.

Use Power Movements and Train Heavy

The ectomorph needs to lift heavy weights to hit the deep muscle fibers that will make the body grow. Don't waste time on isolation or cable movements right now. If you're an ectomorph, you should do the following exercises:

- Legs: Squat, stiff-legged deadlift, donkey calf raise
- Chest: Dumbbell or barbell incline press
- Back: Chin-up; barbell, dumbbell, or T-bar row
- Shoulders: Dumbbell or barbell front press
- Biceps: Barbell or dumbbell curl
- Triceps: Close-grip bench press, dip, lying EZ-bar French press

THE IMPORTANCE OF REST

Ectomorphs tend to train at a fast pace and would benefit greatly—both in recovery and strength—from slowing down. Intense training is the stimulus that creates muscle growth. Intensity can be accomplished in a number of ways; two of the best are lifting heavy and resting longer between sets, and training lighter with shorter rest time.

Because high-intensity workouts are necessary for growth, ectomorphs should focus on lifting heavier and taking longer rest periods between sets to ensure greater muscular recovery for maximum intensity and strength for each set.

Ectomorphs must also give their bodies adequate rest between workouts. The absolute *minimum* rest they need between working the same bodypart is 48 hours. And they should never work a bodypart unless it has *fully* recovered from the previous workout. Because of their high metabolism, ectomorphs should get no less

than 7½ hours (preferably 8 to 9) of sleep every night.

THE NUTRITION FACTOR: EAT, EAT, EAT

Training is unquestionably an important element in the ectomorph's bodybuilding success, but good nutrition is too! In fact, *one of the biggest reasons ectomorphs have so many problems is that they eat too many of the wrong foods and too few of the good foods, and don't eat often enough.*

Let's simplify things. You should structure your diet in the following way:

- Eat five to seven small meals daily.
- Daily protein intake should be 1 to 1.5 grams of protein per pound of bodyweight. It should be no less than 35 percent of your daily total caloric intake.
- Have a protein shake 90 minutes before bedtime.
- Carbs should be 45 percent of daily dietary intake.
- Increase your daily intake of fibrous carbs (cauliflower, broccoli) while limiting your intake of simple sugars (fruits, honey).
- Keep your fat intake to roughly 20 percent of your daily dietary intake.
- Eat slower-burning glycemic index foods such as beans, sweet corn, lentils, yams, peas, nonfat dairy products, porridge, oats, and pasta.
- Supplement your diet with a good multivitamin.
- Drink lots of water throughout the day, at least 80 ounces.

KEEP STRESS LEVELS LOW

Many ectomorphs are high-strung individuals. They're usually amped up and on the go. For such individuals, stress can be a problem because it affects progress in the gym by producing cortisol, a catabolic (yes, the opposite of anabolic) hormone.

Ectomorphs should practice slowing things down and relaxing. Try slowing your pace and taking at least 10 minutes a day to be alone and away from people and noise. In those 10 minutes, lie down or sit in a relaxed position, close your eyes, inhale through your mouth and exhale through your nose, and slowly and softly repeat the words *calm*, *serenity*, and *tranquil*. Feel your muscles relax and become heavy as if concrete weights were attached to them. Imagine that all stress is leaving your body and dissipating in the air. Nothing can bother you. You are in control.

MINIMIZE OUTSIDE ACTIVITIES

Because most ectomorphs have a metabolism as fast as a greyhound's, their bodies tend to burn food very quickly. Many ectomorphs I've talked to complain that they can't put on size. For good reason: they don't eat enough of the right foods, they don't train correctly, and they engage in too much activity.

If you're an ectomorph and your goal is to pack on more size and strength, minimize all other activities outside of weight training. Make sure your body uses all the nutrients you consume to recover and grow from your bodybuilding workouts.

If you must be involved in other physically demanding activities, be sure to take in extra calories—above those you are taking in for bodybuilding—and get plenty of rest. Follow these guidelines and your weight- and strength-gaining problems will be history.

9

Training and Nutrition for the Mesomorph

Blessed be the mesomorphs, those genetically gifted people who seem to gain muscle just by thinking about it. Well, not quite that easily, but mesomorphs are bodybuilding's fastest muscle gainers. Yet despite their propensity to accumulate slabs of muscle in a hurry, mesomorphs need the right training and nutrition program to make the best gains possible.

WHAT IS A MESOMORPH?

The male mesomorph typically is muscular and naturally strong, with a long torso and a big, full chest. The female mesomorph is stronger and more muscular and often more athletic than other women. A mesomorph's strength can increase very quickly, as can muscular size, especially on the right program.

Mesomorphs respond well to training that involves heavy, quick movements along with shaping exercises. The more varied the exercise program, the better the results.

Take quads, for example. After a good warm-up, a mesomorph could begin with a great mass movement like squats, followed by hack squats or leg presses, then a shaping movement like leg extensions.

For hamstrings, the mesomorph might begin with stiff-legged deadlifts, followed by a shaping movement such as standing leg curls. For calves, the first movement might be heavy standing calf raises followed by high-rep toe raises with light weight on the leg press.

THE MORE VARIABLES, THE BETTER

Mesomorphs should make repeated changes in the variables of working out—that is, the number of sets, reps, and exercises; length of training sessions and rest; number of training days; amount of weight used; and exercise angles.

They should also vary training intensity. A combination of three to four weeks of intense training followed by one to two weeks of lower-intensity training seems to promote growth and strength and prevent training burnout.

THE MESOMORPH AND FOOD

Mesomorphs grow best when they get plenty of protein—at least 1 gram per pound of bodyweight daily—and keep carb intake moderately high. The surprising thing about the majority of mesomorphs I know is that they can follow a diet with more than 20 percent of calories from fat (still far less than the typical American diet) and it actually helps them gain mass and strength!

In fact, many mesomorphs can boost their strength levels simply by increasing their fat and protein intake moderately. Strange as it may sound, a tablespoon or two of peanut butter a day can do some amazing things for a mesomorph.

A mesomorph typically will make strength and muscle gains by keeping bodyweight relatively steady, looking to increase muscle mass only gradually. The days of bulking up by 20 or 30 pounds and then cutting down are over for the mesomorphs who want to gain the greatest amount of *quality* lean tissue. In fact, for all individuals, quality muscle size can be gained much more quickly when body fat levels are held under 16 percent for men and 22 percent for women.

THE AEROBIC FACTOR

If building muscle is the goal, intense cardio work such as running should be kept to a minimum. Running long distances can be counterproductive. Many mesomorphs can lose lean muscle tissue quickly if they run over two miles three times weekly.

Some mesomorphs have found wind sprints an excellent way to condition and build the hamstrings, quads, and calves while aerobically conditioning the cardiovascular system.

If running isn't for you, try using the stairclimber, stationary bike, jump rope, or treadmill, or try racket sports or hiking. Just make sure you don't overdo it. Three times per week, 25 to 30 minutes per session (5-minute warm-up, 15 to 20 minutes in your target heart rate zone, 5-minute cool-down), will work well for burning fat. If jumping rope, jump for 3 to 12 minutes and rest only long enough to keep your heart rate in the target zone. In fact, that's the key to doing all your cardiovascular exercise. To find your target heart rate per minute, subtract your age from 220 and multiply by 0.6 and 0.8. That's where you should be exercising aerobically.

Mesomorphs, like endomorphs and ectomorphs, benefit from proper training and nutritional guidelines. Here are a few.

- Using a combination of heavy power movements like squats, deadlifts, rows, and presses with shaping movements like laterals, pressdowns, dumbbell curls, and extensions can give the mesomorph better muscle quality, proportion, and symmetry.
- Mesomorphs respond well to fairly long workouts (up to 80 minutes) and shorter rest between sets (45 to 60 seconds). Staying within the 6-to-10-set and 6-to-12-rep range works well.
- Working out four days a week, such as the two-on, one-off schedule, seems to give the mesomorph's body enough workout frequency and stimulation for growth.

■ A balanced diet is generally good enough for the mesomorph to pack on muscle mass. No need to overload the system with massive amounts of protein or carbs. Eat sensibly and keep the body fat to an acceptable level.

THE OVERMOTIVATION FACTOR

Because the mesomorph can make outstanding gains quickly, some individuals might be inclined to push themselves to the limit. Training intensely is great, but doing too much too quickly can lead to overtraining and injury.

Over the years, the sport of bodybuilding has been rife with genetically gifted mesomorphs with the potential for phenomenal growth and strength. But because of overenthusiasm, they either burned out, injured themselves, or lost motivation to continue training.

If you're a mesomorph, consider yourself fortunate. But be sensible with your training and nutrition. Those two factors will help you reach your bodybuilding potential.

Stay committed to your training. Learn how your body type responds to various training methods, sets, and reps. Structure your training to your body type's needs and you'll be successful.

PART III

The Three Foundational Components

Warming Up, Stretching, and Cooling Down

10

Warming Up

We're going to talk in the next few chapters about three foundational components: warming up, stretching, and cooling down. Let's begin with the warm-up.

THE WARM-UP

In all the years I've been training, I've been very fortunate to have never been injured. I think some regular habits I've established have helped me avoid injury.

- I warm up and stretch before every workout.
- I start with light warm-up sets and stay with the lighter weights until the bodypart I'm working is fully warmed up.
- I use good form for each exercise.
- I immediately stop doing the exercise if I feel any twinge, pain, or abnormal workout discomfort. I will not work a bodypart if I feel any kind of pain in it.

- I stretch the bodypart I've just worked after the last set for that bodypart and for at least 25 seconds per side.

Sure, I've pushed myself too much and have become too sore on lots of occasions, but I quickly learned to never train a bodypart that's still sore until that bodypart is fully recovered and pain free.

The warm-up is really important because it helps raise the core temperature of the body, gets the blood flowing (causing your muscles to perform better and greatly reducing the chance of injury), helps make the muscles more flexible and elastic, gets the joints moving, and lubricates them with synovial fluid (think of it as grease for your joints that helps them move easily).

I've found that certain factors will affect not only my workouts and stretching but my warm-up as well. Temperature is one. Colder weather is tough on the body, and the colder the weather the more time you need to get warmed up for your workout. Conversely, warmer weather is easier on the body and it takes less time to "heat things up on the inside," so to speak.

I've also found that certain times in the day and week are better for me than others, especially the time of day when I train. My best workouts are in the afternoons between 1:00 and 4:00. Interestingly enough, many people have told me that they are more flexible in mid- to late afternoon than mornings or nights. I've tried early morning and late night workouts, but afternoons just feel best to me. However, all of us have our own best time to train, and you'll find it easier, more enjoyable, and more effective if you focus your training, stretching, warm-ups, and cool-downs within that time frame.

PREWORKOUT STRETCH WARM-UP

I like to begin the warm-up with the hands, wrists, and elbows.

1. **Finger stretches:** Open each hand and spread the fingers as wide as possible, then close them. Repeat.
2. **Hand/wrist rotations:** Move your hands and wrists small circles forward and backward.
3. **Elbow bends:** Do body push-outs (just like push-ups) against a dumbbell rack, bench, or wall. This is great for warming up the triceps, too.
4. **Knee-ups:** Stand in place and raise one leg up to your waist. Repeat with the other leg. This is terrific for warming up not only the knees but the quads as well.
5. **Standing bodyweight-only calf raises:** Do 30 to 50 nonstop reps. This really helps stretch and warm up the calves, ankles, and feet.
6. **Standing trunk twists:** With either arm in front of your body, or holding a broomstick behind your neck, twist from side to side for 1 to 3 minutes nonstop.
7. **Jumping:** Jump up and down in place for 30 to 60 seconds.

After doing these stretches I'm ready for the workout. I always begin each exercise with a "mock" set—I go through the exact motions and movement for the exercise I'm about to do, but without weights. I want my body to get settled into the "exercise groove" and my mind and body to be in total synch when the weights are used. Do this and you're going to like what it will do for your workouts.

Now you're ready for the *Bodybuilding 201* stretches in Chapter 11.

11

Stretching

If you like working out and see yourself working out for many years to come, then the best thing you can do (besides training smart, using excellent form, and giving your body plenty of rest) is to stretch. Stretching is even more important as you age because flexibility tends to decrease in those who are older, aren't physically active, or do exercises that work the body in full ranges of motion.

Stretching offers many benefits, including the following:

- Decreases risk of injury
- Reduces stress
- Increases quickness, coordination, flexibility, and agility
- Increases flow of vital nutrients, blood, and synovial fluid to joints and connective tissue
- Decreases muscle soreness, which helps you recover more quickly from workouts

Anyone can and should stretch—it's more than worth any time it takes. Younger people are able to stretch farther and faster than those who are older, so keep that in mind as you gradually build up and work into your ideal stretch program. Also, women are generally more flexible, and thus better stretchers, than men.

THE KINDS OF STRETCHES

Maybe this chapter should be called "Stretching—the Truth," since what you're about to learn are five great ways to stretch and one way that's a big no-no. Here is the first way.

Active Stretching
Think of active stretching (some people call it static-active stretching) as holding a bodypart in the stretched position without any help from any other muscle group. Some examples include yoga positions or holding your leg up off the ground without help from your arms or any other bodypart or muscle group.

You'll find that active stretches will increase your flexibility and strength, but be prepared: this kind of stretching can be intense. Hold the stretch for no more than 20 seconds.

Passive Stretching

Think of passive stretching (some call it static stretching) as relaxed stretching. Passive stretches require help from another muscle group, a partner, or an external fixture or machine. A good example of this would be holding your leg up off the ground using your hand or resting it on a ledge or bench.

You are also passively stretching when you lie down on your back, spread your legs out wide to your sides, and rest your heel on the wall in front of you and keep trying to spread your legs farther and move your heels farther down the wall. When you hold the stretch and don't go any farther, that is considered a passive stretch. When you hold the stretch, then take the stretch a little farther, then hold it again, then take it farther again, and so on, that is considered a static stretch.

PNF Stretching

PNF stands for proprioceptive neuromuscular facilitation. PNF stretches combine isometric and passive stretching and can work wonders in helping you become more flexible.

PNF stretches work by passively stretching a muscle and then contracting that muscle isometrically against resistance while you're in the stretched position, then relaxing for about 25 to 30 seconds, then passively stretching that muscle again a little farther, relaxing again for another 25 to 30 seconds, and so on. Each time you stretch, relax, and stretch again, you're slowly increasing range of motion. You can get even better results from PNF stretching if you have a partner assist you in your stretches.

The following are two safe and very effective PNF stretches:

Hold It, Relax It

Do 1 set, one time only, every three days:

- Do a passive stretch, then slightly relax it.
- Passively stretch again, this time going a little farther, then hold for 20 seconds.
- Relax the muscle for 25 to 30 seconds, and you're finished.

Hold It, Relax It, Flex It

Do 1 set, one time only, every three days:

- Do a passive stretch, then slightly relax it.
- Passively stretch again, this time isometrically contracting it by going a little farther, then hold for 10 to 20 seconds.
- Passively stretch it again, then isometrically contract it by going a little farther than before, then hold for 10 to 20 seconds.
- Relax the muscle for 25 to 30 seconds, and you're finished.

A word of caution: Doctors I've spoken to do not recommend PNF or isometric stretching for children under age 14. Consult your health-care professional to find out whether these, or any other stretches, are right for you.

Dynamic Stretching

This is a favorite type of stretch among martial artists. It involves swinging your torso, arms, and legs in a controlled manner in a small range of motion when you begin and increasing that range of motion as your body warms up.

Always start slowly and easily by doing small arm circles, leg swings, and torso twists. Then slowly widen those circles, use bigger leg swings and twisting farther from side to side until you reach your comfortable range of motion limit.

I like doing these before I begin my workouts. I do wrist and hand circles, arm circles, standing alternat-

RESEARCH UPDATE: Does Stretching Prevent Soreness?

"The next morning I couldn't even lift my arm to comb my hair. Each time I tried, pain shot through every muscle in my shoulder and arm. I couldn't hold the comb. I tried to drink coffee and spilled it all over the table. I was helpless."

—Arnold Schwarzenegger, about the day after his first-ever workout

It's common for many people, especially when they're just starting an exercise program, to feel sore for the next day or two after exercise. We're always told to spend a lot of time stretching immediately after exercise to prevent delayed-onset muscle soreness (DOMS). But does it really help?

Not according to a team of Danish researchers. They found that stretching before and after exercise has no effect on muscle soreness. The researchers persuaded seven healthy but untrained women to take part in two experiments.*

During the first experiment, the women exercised their right quadriceps to exhaus-tion. Ratings of muscle pain were taken for the next seven days. In experiment two, the women performed the same type of exercise. This time, however, they spent 90 seconds stretching before and after exer-cise. Again, muscle pain was assessed for seven days.

For these women, stretching had no effect on muscle soreness, which reached a peak two days after exercise. So what actually causes the soreness? A bout of exercise causes inflammation, which leads to an increase in the production of immune cells (composed mostly of macro-phages and neutrophils). Levels of these immune cells reach a peak 24 to 48 hours after exercise. These cells, in turn, produce bradykinins and prostaglandins, which make the pain receptors in your body more sensitive. The result? Whenever you move, these pain receptors are stimulated. Because they're far more sensitive to pain than normal, you end up feeling sore. Now, this doesn't mean that you shouldn't stretch after exercise. But if you're doing it to ease muscle soreness, there's little evidence to show it makes any real difference.

* Lund, H., P. Vestergaard-Poulsen, I. L. Kanstrup, and P. Sejrsen. "The Effect of Passive Stretching on Delayed-Onset Muscle Soreness, and Other Detrimental Effects Following Eccentric Exercise." *Scandinavian Journal of Medicine and Science in Sports* 8 (1998): 216–21.

ing knee-ups, trunk twists, jumping in place, and stretches for any other bodypart/area that needs a good warm-up before hitting the weights.

Isometric Stretching

Think of isometric stretching as stretching a bodypart or muscle group and then holding it in that position until the stretch is finished. Many believe that isometric stretching is one of the quickest and best ways to develop greater flexibility and is far more effective than either passive stretching or active stretching alone. Isometric stretching is good for gain-ing more strength in the contracted muscles.

A good example of an isometric stretch is one I described earlier in this chapter: lie on your back on the floor and put your legs up, resting your heels against the wall in front of your body. Stretch your legs out to each side (with your heels still on the wall) as far as you can, then hold that position without resting or relaxing the stretched muscle.

Whether you use a wall, a machine, a partner, or anything else to help you, when you isometrically stretch you want to get in a stretched position and hold that position. Try to hold each isometric stretch for about 10 seconds. And only one isometric stretch set per bodypart or muscle

group every three days should work
great.

Ballistic Stretching

I saved this type of stretching for last
because it's the one I *do not* want you
to do. Ballistic stretching has injured
many people. It uses the momentum or
weight of a part of the torso (upper or
lower) to force it beyond its normal
range of motion. This can be incredibly unsafe for your body.

Ballistic stretching is simply a
fancy term for essentially bouncing
into and out of a stretched position.
This uses the muscles you're stretching
as a sort of spring or coil to propel you
out of the stretched position and back
up again. The sudden impact, force,
and pressure this kind of stretch puts
on your relaxed muscles can be brutal.

Think of how it would feel (and
what kind of damage you'd do to
your body) if one morning someone
dropped a 500-pound barbell on your
back just as you got out of bed and
stood up, forcing your leg muscles to
instantly tighten, massively contract,
and rip, tear, pull, and snap (connective tissue, too). Ballistic stretching
puts so much force—all at once—on
muscle and connective tissue that the
body has no choice but to stop the
insanity by injuring itself so that you
won't do it again. So let's not even go
down that road. Let's make it a *Bodybuilding 201* stretching rule: No ballistic stretching. Period.

PRE- AND POSTWORKOUT STRETCHING

Back and Lats

Chin Bar Hang

The chin bar hang works great for
stretching those lats. Take an overhand
grip on either a chin bar or Smith
machine bar with the bar racked at the

Chin bar hang

highest position on the machine. The
preferred way is to use a bar that's high
enough for your entire body to hang
straight up and down without your
feet touching the floor. If this is not
possible, then do these with your
knees bent and your calves and feet
behind you.

The key is to let your arms fully
extend and your upper body hang so
the lats will be stretched. Hang in this
position for at least 20 seconds. If your
grip will allow, hang a few seconds
longer.

Vertical Bar Grab

Using one arm at a time, grab a vertical bar on a machine, lean back, and

Vertical bar grab

Lat pulldown stretch

hold the stretched position for 20 to 30 seconds. Really feel it stretch those lats. You'll also feel a stretch in your biceps. Repeat for the other side.

Lat Pulldown Stretch

This exercise is somewhat like the chin bar hang, but it uses a straight bar with stirrup handles at the ends. You could also use a regular straight bar with a wide overhand grip.

Position yourself as if you were preparing to do lat pulldowns. Once you grab the bar and your arms are fully extended overhead, keep them there for 20 to 30 seconds. To feel it even more, lean slightly forward.

To increase the stretch, use a heavy weight—I suggest using a weight that's equal to your bodyweight. If it's too light you won't feel it; too heavy, and you won't be able to pull the bar down far enough so you can sit down.

Chest

Pec Deck

For this stretch you'll use the pec deck for support. Position yourself with arms behind you and resting against the vertical pec deck pads, just like you would if you were doing the exercise. But instead of keeping your upper body firm against the back pad, let your upper body come forward,

Pec deck

Vertical bar push

keeping your arms in place against the pec deck pads, and keep leaning forward until your arms are behind you and you really feel the chest stretch. Hold the position for 20 to 30 seconds.

Vertical Bar Push

Grab a vertical bar on a machine with one arm. Keep your upper body erect. With your arm locked, turn your upper body away from the arm holding the vertical bar. You should feel a stretch in the pecs. Hold the position for 20 to 30 seconds, then repeat on the other side.

Cable Crossover

You'll use the beginning phase of a cable crossover exercise for this stretch. Position your body in the middle of a pulley station. With your left hand grab the stirrup-style handle connected to the left upper pulley, and with your right hand grab the stirrup-style handle connected to the right upper pulley. Choose a weight that's roughly 25 percent of your body-weight (for example, if you weigh 200 pounds, use 50 pounds on both weight stacks).

Allow your arms and the cables to fully extend up and out to your sides until you feel a really nice stretch in your chest. To feel it even more, move your upper body slightly forward while your arms are fully extended. Hold this position for 20 to 30 seconds.

Cable crossover

Triceps

Opposite-Arm Grab

Extend your right arm directly overhead. While keeping your upper arm
close to your head, bend your elbow so
that your forearm and hand are bent
over behind the arm. With your left
hand, grab your right elbow and gently
push down on it. You should feel a
stretch in the triceps. Hold the position for 20 to 30 seconds, then repeat
on the other side.

Vertical Bar Triceps Push

Lean one side of your upper body
against a vertical machine bar and let
that side's triceps lie flat against the
bar. Try to place as much of your upper
arm as possible firmly against the

Opposite-arm grab (a)

Opposite-arm grab (b)

Vertical bar triceps push

vertical bar. Bend your elbow so that your forearm and hand are bent behind the arm. Lean into the vertical bar until you really feel your triceps stretch. Hold the position for 20 to 30 seconds, then repeat on the other side.

Lowered EZ-Bar

If you can do the lying EZ-bar French press, then you'll easily be able to do this stretch. In fact, that's exactly the exercise you'll use, except instead of lowering the weight behind your head and extending it back up overhead, you'll simply lower the weight and maintain the lowered position for 20 to 30 seconds. Remember to keep the upper arms in a locked position and the hands lowered as far as possible to really make the triceps stretch.

Lowered EZ-bar

Biceps

Straight-Arm Twist-Out

Do this quick and simple stretch immediately after your set in your biceps workout. Stand up straight with your arms hanging straight down at your sides. Turn your hands (be sure the hands are open and the fingers are pointing downward) so that your palms are facing out and away from your body and the backs of your hands are facing the sides of your body. Hold the position for 20 to 30 seconds.

Vertical Bar Biceps Push

Place the back of your hand against the vertical bar on a machine, keeping your arm completely straight. Keeping your upper body erect and your arm locked, slowly turn your upper body away from the bar. The more you turn your body away from the bar, the more you should feel the stretch in the

Straight-arm twist-out (a)

Straight-arm twist-out (b)

Vertical bar biceps push

biceps. Hold the position for 20 to 30 seconds, then repeat on the other side.

Shoulders and Delts

Opposite-Elbow Pull

You can do this shoulder stretch in a standing or sitting position. Bring your right arm across the front of your body

Opposite-elbow pull

toward your left shoulder. As it is coming across your front, grab your right elbow with your left hand and slowly pull it across your body and toward your left side. You will feel a good stretch in the right shoulder.

Either hold the stretch for 10 seconds or do what I do: hold it for 2 to 3 seconds, then release; stretch again for 2 to 3 seconds, then release; finally, stretch for a third time for 2 to 3 seconds. Repeat on the other side and you've just done a safe, simple, and very effective shoulder stretch.

Quads

Flat Bench Kneel

Find a padded flat bench. Kneel down on top of the bench so that your legs are together and your glutes and upper-body weight are resting on top of your calves, which are together and underneath you.

Keep your upper body in a straight line and slowly allow your upper torso to shift backward until you

Flat bench kneel

feel the stretch in your quads and upper thighs. Hold this position for 20 to 30 seconds. The more your upper body leans back toward your feet, the more you'll feel it in the quads. To reduce the stretch, simply come up and forward.

Standing One-Leg Hold

Stand up straight. Bend one knee until your calf and foot are behind you. With the hand on the side of the bent leg, grab the top of your foot and hold it until the heel touches your glutes. Keep the bent upper leg in a straight line with your upper body. To increase the stretch, tip the pelvis forward. Hold the position for 20 to 30 seconds, then repeat on the other side.

Bodyweight Deep Squat Bend

Think of how you'd do a barbell squat—body upright, head up and looking forward, upper-body weight centered over the back of the heels, knees traveling in a straight line over

Bodyweight deep squat bend (a)

Standing one-leg hold

Bodyweight deep squat bend (b)

the big toes, feet about shoulder-width apart. That's the position you'll use for this stretch, only you're not going to use any weight, just a good deep knee bend. Lower your body until you reach the bottom position of the knee bend/squat and stay in the lowered position for 20 to 30 seconds.

Hamstrings

Ankle Grab

Keep both legs together and feet pointed straight forward. Bend forward at the waist until your chest comes down to upper-leg level and your head is at knee level. Grab your ankles and with a gentle but controlled pull bring your upper body down as far as possible until you feel a great stretch in your hamstrings. Don't bounce. Simply go as far as you comfortably can and

you'll find your range of motion improving as you include this stretch in your routine on a regular basis.

Stiff-Legged Deadlift with Bottom Pause

For this stretch, go through the motion of a dumbbell or barbell stiff-legged deadlift. Holding the weight with your arms locked down against your legs and your body fully erect, bend the upper torso over until the barbell is lowered as far as possible. Pause for 2 to 3 seconds in the bottom position, then return the upper torso to the starting erect position.

How far down should you go? Simply lower your upper body as far as possible until you feel a great stretch in your hamstrings. Some people will be able to lower the bar until it

Ankle grab

Stiff-legged deadlift with bottom pause

touches the top of their feet. Others may be able to bring the barbell down only to shin level. Bend your knees if you must, but only slightly. Make sure the hamstrings are fully stretched. Don't bounce. Go as far as you comfortably can and you'll find your range of motion improving as you include this stretch in your routine on a regular basis.

Try not to round your back too much as you lower the weight. Keep it tight, as this is not a lat movement. Keep the bar in the lowered position for 2 to 3 seconds. Keep both legs together and feet pointed straight forward.

Remember that the farther the weights are in front of your body and legs, the *less* you'll feel the stretch in the hamstrings. The closer you bring the weight to the shins and lower legs, the *more* you'll feel it in the hamstrings.

Calves

Standing Lowered Heel
This is an easy one. Simply stand on the edge of a platform that's high enough that your heels can come down as far as your range of motion allows without touching the floor. Keep your body straight, and hold on to something for balance only if you need to; be careful not to take your bodyweight off the stretched calf muscles. It is best to work both calves at the same time. This will really burn, and that's exactly what you want. Hold the stretched position for 20 to 30 seconds.

Leg Press Toe Raise
Place the balls of your feet on the bottom edge of the foot platform on a leg press machine. Keep your knees locked. Moving only the ankles, let

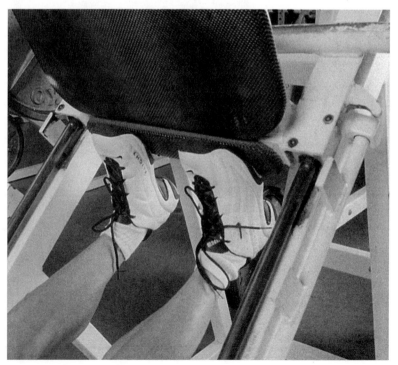

Standing lowered heel

Leg press toe raise

your feet come back and the platform come down as far as you comfortably can. Hold the feet in this stretched position for 1 to 2 seconds. Then, keeping your knees locked, push the weight back up as far as you can with your feet. Hold the weight in this fully contracted position for 1 to 2 seconds and repeat. Go for high reps of more than 20 per set.

Leaning Against Wall

Stand up straight. Place one or both hands against a wall. With your upper

body upright, bring your right leg back about 2 to 3 feet behind you and place the entire surface of your left foot firmly on the floor. Lean forward slightly until you feel a good stretch in the left calf. The farther forward your upper body goes, the more you'll feel the stretch in the left calf. Hold for 20 to 30 seconds and repeat on the other side.

Leaning against wall with two hands

Leaning against wall with one hand

12

Cooling Down

The first component of our workout was the warm-up. The second component was stretching. Now I will address the third and final component: the cool-down. I like to combine three components of my cool-down: peak contractions, stretches, and then massage.

The peak contraction part of it is easy and quick. Simply pick an exercise movement you'd do for a bodypart, then, without any weights, squeeze, flex, and contract that bodypart just as if you were performing that movement and hold it in the fully contracted position as intensely as you can for 3 to 6 seconds, then stretch it.

The massage part of the cooldown can be as simple as rubbing the worked muscle for 15 to 45 seconds or as indulgent as arranging for a professional massage after the workout. Besides just feeling great, massage is actually really good for your body. It helps increase blood flow and circulation, thereby helping your body get rid of lactic acid and possibly minimizing postworkout soreness.

RESEARCH UPDATE: Burning Calories After Your Workout

Researchers from the University of Tasmania have revealed why some people burn more calories after exercise than others, even when they do exactly the same type of workout.*

Your consumption of oxygen, and hence the number of calories you burn, tends to rise after exercise. Although it used to be known as oxygen debt, more recent studies have named it EPOC, which is short for excess postexercise oxygen consumption.

The effect of EPOC on fat loss is a controversial topic, mainly because the duration of EPOC seems to vary so much from study to study. Some papers report that EPOC lasts for just one hour, while others have recorded EPOC lasting two days. However, this Australian study explains why EPOC seems to vary so much. The trial, published in the *European Journal of Applied Physiology*, shows that the amount of muscle you have directly influences how long EPOC lasts.

Eight male and eight female physical education students took part in the study. They performed three different trials, with each trial separated by one week.

- During the first trial, test subjects exercised for 30 minutes at 40 percent of their aerobic capacity.
- In trial two, they exercised for 30 minutes at 50 percent of their aerobic capacity.
- Trial three involved exercise at 70 percent of aerobic capacity.

Oxygen consumption was then measured for several hours after exercise. Because the expenditure of calories and oxygen consumption are closely linked, the researchers were able to estimate how many calories were burned after exercise.

The men continued to burn more calories for almost 50 minutes after finishing the workout. However, postexercise calorie expenditure in women lasted for only 40 minutes. But here's where things get interesting. When the figures were adjusted to take into account the fact that men have more muscle, variations between the males and females vanished. In other words, the more muscle you have, the more calories you burn after your workout.

One of the main benefits of lifting weights when you're trying to lose fat is the preservation of lean muscle tissue. For example, if you use just aerobic exercise and diet to help you lose weight, roughly 2 out of every 10 pounds you lose comes from muscle. This has the effect of blunting the normal rise in caloric expenditure after exercise, making further weight loss increasingly difficult.

In short, any form of resistance exercise contributes to weight loss in one of two ways. First, the workout itself helps to create a calorie deficit. Second, by preserving lean muscle, you'll continue to burn calories long after exercise.

---

* Smith, J., and L. McNaughton. "The Effects of Intensity of Exercise on Excess Post-Exercise Oxygen Consumption and Energy Expenditure in Moderately Trained Men and Women." *European Journal of Applied Physiology* 67 (1993): 420–25.

PART IV

The Great Leap Forward

13

How to Keep Getting Great Results

If only you could grow and get stronger workout after workout, life would be wonderful, wouldn't it? But the reality is that the longer you've been training and the bigger and stronger you get, the harder it is to keep getting bigger and stronger.

Everyone's body has built-in genetic limits to its size and strength. While you can do a lot to come close to reaching that limit, the body reaches a certain set point at which growth and strength really slow down and may even stop.

For a lot of people, this is very frustrating because all those years of fast gains have spoiled them and tricked them into thinking those results will never end. And when that frustration sets in, people often search for anything that will get things going again, like supplements or even illegal drugs.

But those are quick fixes. If you're getting results by taking supplements, you'll have to *keep* taking them to keep getting results. Even so, the body quickly gets used to the amount of supplement you're taking and slows down its response to that supplement. Then you've either got to keep taking more and more of the supplement or try something different that the body hasn't built up a tolerance to.

It's the same with drugs, only with more dangerous consequences. Drugs are powerful substances that change body chemistry in the short term. If you take too much or take them too often or for too long, you can become addicted and possibly cause your body's chemicals to change long term or even shut down. I've heard stories of people going the chemical route, and it's caused them major problems with the liver, other organs, and hormones.

Consider the way drugs work. In the beginning, it takes only a small amount of the drug to get good results. Then it takes more of the substance, yet results begin to diminish. Finally, you have to take larger and larger amounts of the drug—for longer and longer times—and the results keep diminishing until you're hooked, out of money, or injured (because drugs do mask the pain that often shows up only after the drug is stopped), which will ultimately keep you from getting *any* results.

WHAT TO DO

I've always believed that while it may take longer, whatever gains in size and strength you build *naturally*, you'll

keep. Not only that, you'll keep the gains longer than someone who doesn't do it that way. I've met many bodybuilders who've used unnatural means to put on gigantic size and strength, but once they stopped using the aids that helped them get big and strong they went down to their smaller versions. Make that *much* smaller versions.

I was lucky that I had some good influences when I began my training. One of them was a man in his 50s, about 5'6", who had over 20-inch calves (a genetic natural), could easily bench press more than 400 pounds, and came from the old school of basic training, using a combination of body-building, powerlifting, and Olympic lifts in his workouts.

He gave me lots of great advice that I've never forgotten, and it was that advice, along with many of the things I'm telling you in this book, that helped me to put on over 60 pounds of muscle in two years, all of it naturally, training three to four times a week, eating four to five meals a day, and having a protein shake at night before bed. I've never used any drugs, and my body stays big and strong year after year. Not only that, but the small amount of training (and even with light weights) needed to maintain that size and strength today would astonish you.

WHAT'S THE POINT?

It's simple, really. The answer is to train smart, train consistently, and do it naturally by using some techniques and principles that'll allow you to keep progressing when others stop. You need techniques and principles that will keep you healthy, big, and strong year after year, that will keep your workouts fun and exciting, that will keep the motivating fire burning inside you. One of these principles is time compression.

Time Compression

Think of this as training more effectively in less time. For example, let's take a workout that lasts 30 minutes. The goal would be to reduce that training time to less than 30 minutes, and here's how you can do it:

- Do more reps but fewer sets.
- Do more sets but fewer reps.
- Do fewer exercises but increase reps and sets.
- Do lighter weights with faster reps with more sets.
- Do heavier weights with faster reps with fewer sets.
- Do more exercises but with fewer sets and reps and less time between sets and exercises.

No matter which option you choose to shorten your workout, be sure to make the time you do spend worthwhile.

14

Reverse Progression Training

Much of the weight training wisdom you first learn says to go heavier at the beginning of your workout when you're strongest and then decrease the weight on each succeeding set as you become weaker. Nothing wrong with that. But I'm going to have you try something different: *go heavier as you get weaker*. Two things to keep in mind as you do this:

1. You won't be able to do as many reps for each set as you'll do in your earlier sets.
2. You should use a spotter or training partner to help you (that is, *barely* help you) complete any reps you cannot complete on your own.

This type of training, when used sparingly, will force your body to tap into its deep reserves and force it to use those deep muscle fibers and endurance ability that can take your body and workouts to a new level. But be warned: this is tough stuff and the technique should not be used too often or too much in any workout.

I suggest doing one complete week of this type of training every eight weeks.

THE PROGRESSIVE OVERLOAD MYTH

When you first set foot in the gym, chances are that you did it because you wanted to improve or change something about your body—to make it either stronger, leaner, fitter, or healthier.

However, if you've been training for some time, you know that your rate of progress gradually slows down. To combat this, many people simply add more weight to the barbell or spend longer in the gym. Unfortunately, it's just not that simple.

According to popular legend, the ancient Greek strongman Milo began carrying a young calf on his shoulders each day. As the animal grew, Milo also grew stronger. Eventually, he was able to carry a fully grown bull.

And so the concept of gradual progressive overload was born.

According to this principle, you need to constantly increase the demands you impose on your body in order to make it bigger, stronger, or leaner.

Let's say that you're training with the main goal of building muscle size and strength. In theory, all you need to do is pick an exercise and choose a resistance you can lift for a certain number of repetitions. Then, as soon as you're able to increase the number of repetitions, you add a few pounds of weight to the bar. For instance, you might be able to squat 200 pounds for a maximum of 10 repetitions. If you added even 5 pounds of weight to the bar each month, you'd be squatting with 260 pounds just one year from now. Continue the process for the next five years, and you'll be squatting 500 pounds.

If you've been working out for more than a few months, you probably realize that this kind of continuous progress just doesn't happen—no matter how hard you train, how many supplements you use, or how much "positive thinking" you do. In short, the principle of gradual progressive overload is highly overrated.

Of course, the speed at which you progress depends on several factors, such as your genes, age, lifestyle, and eating habits. It also depends on a principle known as the ceiling of adaptation. What this means is that the closer you are to your muscle growth "ceiling," the slower your gains will be.[1] Someone with five years of training under his or her belt is a lot nearer the ceiling of adaptation than someone who is just starting out.

PERIODIZATION

If you have reached a point where you feel like you're making little or no progress, an easy way to improve your results is simply to alternate between heavy and lighter training days. For example, you might decide to train your upper body twice each week. During the first workout, you would use a weight that limits you to 4 to 6 repetitions, with longer periods of rest (2 to 3 minutes) between sets. During the lighter workout, you would use slightly higher repetitions (8 to 12) with a shorter period of rest (60 seconds) between sets. This type of training, called nonlinear periodization, is a great way to stimulate new gains in strength and size. Varying your workouts in this way will also keep you interested and reduce boredom, which is vital if you want to make exercise a lifelong habit.

---

1 Kraemer, W. J., K. Adams, E. Cafarelli, G. A. Dudley, C. Dooly, M. S. Feigenbaum, S. J. Fleck, B. Franklin, A. C. Fry, J. R. Hoffman, R. U. Newton, J. Potteiger, M. H. Stone, N. A. Ratamess, and T. Triplett-McBride. "American College of Sports Medicine Position Stand: Progression Models in Resistance Training for Healthy Adults." *Medicine and Science in Sports and Exercise* 34 (2002): 364–80.

15

Strategies for Success

One of the most powerful ways to get better results is by keeping your workouts intense. There are lots of ways to do that, and here is a good one if you're short on time.

THE 3-30-3 MODIFIED WORKOUT

Before they graduated from school, got a different job, had a family, or experienced other life changes that took their time, many people used to be able to train long and often, and they got great results. But life happens, and things happen that limit our time. So what can you do if you're short on time but long on desire to get an intense and effective workout? You can try the 3-30-3 modified workout. The gist of this workout is training the whole body three times a week. Pick any three days you want, but there must be a complete day of rest between workouts. The second component of the 3-30-3 workout is the use of 3 sets per bodypart. They can be any of the following:

- 1 set of three different exercises per bodypart
- 2 sets of one exercise and 1 set of another exercise for that same bodypart
- 3 sets of the same exercise for that bodypart

It's your choice, and I suggest mixing it up each time you work out to keep it interesting.

The third component of the workout is resting 30 seconds between each exercise, each set, and each bodypart in the workout. That means that if you're training chest and you're doing 1 set of three exercises for your chest, you could do it like this:

- Do 25- to 35-degree dumbbell incline presses for the first exercise
- Rest 30 seconds
- Do dumbbell incline flyes with only a slight incline for the second exercise
- Rest 30 seconds
- Do across-the-bench dumbbell pullovers for the third exercise
- Rest 30 seconds

Then move on to working your back and so on. Make this workout brief and intense, and if you're tight on time it could be exactly what you need to stay big, strong, happy, and healthy.

THE MORE/LESS SPLIT

It's a fact that all of us have some bodyparts that grow and respond better than others. Yet even with the bodypart that grows quickly, one side of you grows faster and is stronger than the other. That's why you should try the more/less split.

The key word in bodybuilding and training is *balance*. You want your body to look symmetrical and each bodypart to be equally strong. With the more/less split, you identify which bodypart and side need to be increased in size and strength, and then you adjust your training to give that lacking bodypart and side the extra train-

---

RESEARCH UPDATE:
Gaining Weight

With the mass of conflicting opinions, weight gain supplements, and "secret" Bulgarian training programs, it's no wonder many people are confused about how to gain weight.

Unfortunately, when you're trying to figure out how to gain weight, it's easy to ignore the most important limiting factor—your genetics. Specifically, scientists have isolated one particular gene that, through a protein called myostatin, actually slows your rate of muscle growth. Not only does myostatin affect the rate at which you gain weight, it can also slow the gain in fat that normally occurs as you get older. In simple terms, if you want to gain weight in the form of muscle, the less myostatin, the better.

Much of the early research on myostatin has been conducted in animals. In mice in which myostatin has been "knocked out," individual muscles weigh twice as much as those of normal mice. This increase in muscle size seems to be a combination of muscle-fiber hyperplasia (an increase in the number of muscle fibers) and hypertrophy (an increase in the size of those fibers).

More interesting still, researchers from the University of Maryland have shown that myostatin affects muscle growth in women, too.* The study tracked a group of men and women taking part in a weight-training program for nine weeks. Muscle growth in the quadriceps was measured at the end of the study.

Analyzing the results, the research team found that the myostatin genotype didn't appear to be responsible for the different rates of muscle growth between men and women (the increase in muscle volume in the thigh was twice as great in the men). However, when only the women were analyzed, muscle growth in those with the *less common* myostatin genotype was almost 70 percent greater.

Variations in myostatin genotype could explain why some people gain weight in the form of muscle far more quickly than others. Muscle fibers in elite bodybuilders, for example, are often no bigger than those of someone who has never picked up a barbell. Their muscles are larger because they contain a greater number of small- to average-sized fibers.

Hyperplasia (remember, hyperplasia describes an increase in the number rather than the size of muscle fibers) may be more likely to occur in bodybuilders with a less common myostatin genotype. This could be one of the reasons—apart from drugs—they gain weight so quickly. Of course, we'll need more studies with larger numbers in each genotype group to figure out whether this is true. However, these results do show that genetic variations among individuals have a big influence on muscle growth.

The bottom line is that many of the "extreme" physiques you see in the magazines are far more likely to be the result of favorable genetics than the particular training program or food supplement they *claim* to be using.

---

* Ivey, F. M., S. M. Roth, R. E. Ferrell, B. L. Tracy, J. T. Lemmer, D. E. Hurlbut, G. F. Martel, E. L. Siegel, J. L. Fozard, E. Jeffrey Metter, J. L. Fleg, and B. F. Hurley. "Effects of Age, Gender, and Myostatin Genotype on the Hypertrophic Response to Heavy Resistance Strength Training." *Journals of Gerontology Series A: Biological Sciences and Medical Sciences* 55 (2000): M641–M648.

ing it needs to become balanced with the other. This can be accomplished by doing more sets, more reps, and even heavier weights for that side (wherever practical) each time you work that bodypart until it reaches equal balance with the other side.

And it won't take long for it to catch up, either. Most bodyparts that need extra work are only slightly weaker and smaller than the other, so it shouldn't take you much time to make it happen. Try 1 or 2 extra sets for the weaker side for 30 to 60 days, and that should help.

THE EUROBLAST

I love traveling to Europe. It seems that every time I go there I pick up a new little twist on training. One of those twists that I've enjoyed using is something I call the EuroBlast. The Euro-Blast is all about pumping the muscles in different ways and suffusing the bodypart you're working with massive quantities of blood and nutrients. And it's not just doing a regular barbell curl, in the regular way, until the arm gets tired. What you want is to use that muscle as intensely as possible.

RESEARCH UPDATE:
Workout Routines

Do you ever skip workout routines because you don't have the time for those long, boring bouts of exercise the experts say you need? If so, a research team from the University of Pittsburgh School of Medicine has some good news.

The study, led by assistant professor John M. Jakicic, shows that workout routines involving shorter bouts of exercise make it far more likely you'll stick to your program. What's more, workout programs involving shorter bouts of exercise were actually more effective at promoting weight loss, challenging the conventional view that you need to exercise for at least 20 minutes before you start burning fat.

Overweight females were split into two groups. Both groups were assigned to one of two different workout routines. Group one performed a single bout of exercise. Group two performed several bouts of exercise each day, with each bout lasting just 10 minutes. In addition to their workout programs, the women also followed a low-calorie diet, consuming 1,200 to 1,500 calories each day.

Results showed that the workout program involving several 10-minute bouts of exercise actually improved adherence and increased weight loss. The women who split their workouts were able to train more regularly, exercising 30 percent more often than subjects completing a single bout of exercise. They also exercised longer, recording an impressive 224 minutes of exercise per week—36 minutes more than the women in group one. Although gains in aerobic fitness were similar between the two groups, women using the shorter bouts of exercise actually lost more weight. During the 20-week study, they shed 20 pounds, compared to just 14 pounds in group one.

One of the main reasons many people feel the need to exercise for longer periods is the myth that it takes 20 minutes before you start burning fat. Although the number of fat calories your body uses for fuel does increase the longer you spend exercising, the key to losing fat is simply to burn more calories than you eat. So it doesn't matter whether you burn the calories in one long workout or several shorter ones.

As this study shows, both approaches are effective for anyone wanting to lose weight. It's also worth pointing out that multiple bouts of exercise lead to a progressively greater rise in growth hormone levels. In other words, growth hormone is generally higher in the third workout of the day than it is in the first. One of the roles of growth hormone is to promote the breakdown of stored fat. So it's possible that the first bout of exercise "primes" your body to burn more fat calories in bouts two and three.

In short, if you don't have time to squeeze in one long workout, you might want to try several shorter ones. Ten minutes of brisk walking in the morning, 10 minutes in the afternoon, and 10 minutes in the evening work just as well as one longer bout of exercise lasting 30 minutes.

The EuroBlast should be used in different ways. Here are a few that I've found effective:

- Pick one exercise and do only 1 set, and don't count reps. Simply keep the weight moving up and down until that bodypart reaches peak pump.
- When using it on the last exercise in a series of multiple sets and exercises for a bodypart, do short-range reps (moving the weight only 3 to 6 inches up and down) until the muscle is no longer able to move the weight.
- Have a partner help you force 5 to 7 more reps after you've reached muscular failure, then rack the weight. Have your partner strip off 40 to 60 percent of the weight. Do another 5 to 7 reps with your partner's help.
- Do 2, 3, or 4 of these "rack-and-strip" pumping sets. Have the partner strip off 20 percent of the weight for the first set, then another 20 percent on the second set, and then another 20 percent for the third set until you've reached the 60 percent reduction.

The key to the EuroBlast is to keep the muscle moving and the blood flowing to achieve a great pump.

THE ASIAN ARSENAL

Another place I've spent a good deal of time visiting is Asia, having lived in Japan for the better part of a year. Many of the Asian bodybuilders I've met are also martial artists, and they've found that although it's desirable to be quick when they punch or kick, it's even more desirable to have plenty of power behind those punches and kicks.

Bodybuilders are not known as athletes with great flexibility or endurance, yet these Asian bodybuilder/martial artists are. You might want to try some of their techniques.

The Asian arsenal takes the basic exercises you already know how to do and adds the flexibility, speed, endurance, and resistance components to them. Some examples include punching with dumbbells in each hand, kicking with leg weights around ankles, sweeping arm movements with wrist weights, brisk walking on the treadmill, or using ankle and wrist weights while working out on the stairclimber or riding a bike.

The amount of resistance isn't as important as having *some* resistance constantly on your body when you exercise. It's when you're finished with that exercise and you take the weights off that you notice a huge difference in your speed and agility.

The only place I'd not add much resistance would be around the waist. Many people have discovered that the obliques/trunk muscles can develop very quickly—and once developed, that's a muscle area that doesn't want to get smaller and can make your waist bigger than you want. It's fine to use weights around arms, ankles, and wrists.

Great martial artists don't need to be big or powerlifting-kind of strong. Look at Bruce Lee, who was in the 135-pound range but was amazingly strong and fast. Just adding a little resistance to your body can give you more endurance, speed, and strength, changing the way your body looks and feels.

RESEARCH UPDATE:
High-Speed Training

If you're looking for a new way to add variety to your weight training program, try varying your lifting speed. The standard advice on repetition speed is to use only slow, controlled movements. This advice does work for many people. However, a weight training program that includes subtle variations in repetition speed can lead to big changes in the composition of your muscles.

The muscles in your body consist of thousands of tiny muscle fibers. These fibers are broadly classed as either fast-twitch or slow-twitch muscle fibers. Your body "recruits" different fibers depending on the type of exercise you perform. Fast-twitch muscle fibers are better suited for short bouts of high-intensity activity (such as a 40-meter sprint). Slow-twitch muscle fibers are ideal for low-intensity, long-duration activity (such as long-distance running).

A recent study published in the *European Journal of Applied Physiology* compared the effects of two different training programs. Each program involved arm curls performed three times each week for 10 weeks. One group of subjects used fast movements, while the second group used slower movements.

In the subjects using fast movements, there was an increase in the percentage of fast-twitch fibers and a decrease in the percentage of slow-twitch fibers. There were no significant changes in fiber types in subjects who trained using slower movements.

The increase in the percentage of fast-twitch muscle fibers seen in this study suggests that these fibers were activated to a greater extent during the fast movements rather than the slow ones.

Fast-twitch fibers are normally recruited when you lift an extremely heavy weight. They also "take over" when slow-twitch fibers become fatigued. However, fast-twitch fibers are also recruited during high-speed trained movements that use lighter weights.

To make things even more confusing, fast-twitch fibers can be divided into type IIA and type IIB (with more recent studies showing a type IIC, and even a type IIAB and type IIAC).

Muscle fibers are a highly "plastic" substance. They can alter their characteristics depending on the type of training you do. This study reported an increase in the percentage of type IIB muscle fibers. However, it's worth pointing out that the training involved fast eccentric movements (the eccentric phase usually describes the "lowering" part of an exercise).

Although high-speed eccentric training can stimulate muscle adaptation, the high risk of injury means that it's probably safer to use faster movements during the lifting part of an exercise, rather than the lowering.

This doesn't mean you should use faster lifting speeds all the time. Certain exercises, such as the squat, bench press, or power clean, are better suited to high-speed training. Movements designed to isolate smaller muscle groups, like the triceps kickback or concentration curl, are better suited to slower lifting speeds.

It's also important to note that high-speed training has the potential to cause injury and should be avoided until you're confident you can perform the exercise correctly. You'll also need to warm up with several light "practice" sets before using a heavier weight.

Because it's typically used to develop muscle strength (rather than muscle size), high-speed training usually involves multiple sets per exercise (3 to 6 sets), low repetitions (1 to 5 repetitions per set), and long rest times between sets (3 to 5 minutes).

One important point: If you decide to include high-speed exercises in your training program, make sure you have a solid "base" of training behind you—high-speed training definitely isn't for beginners.

16

Secrets of a 700-Pound Bench Presser

When I started working out, people would always ask me, "How much can you bench?" It appeared that the bench press was *the* exercise that told the world just how big and strong you were. And it always seemed like the guys who were shorter and had shorter arms could bench press more than taller guys with longer arms, who had a longer way to lower that weight and push it back up.

Many bodybuilders try really hard to get their strength up on the bench press, and some of them do it right. But many of them do it incorrectly and manage to eke out only a few pounds more. And this is after lots of sweat, many workouts, and long hours in the gym. It can be very frustrating.

One of the world champion athletes I've interviewed over the years was a guy named Ken Lain from Texas. Sure, boys from Texas are known to be big and strong, but Ken Lain wasn't just your average Texan. He was a guy who could bench press over 700 pounds!

In fact, before he retired from competition, Ken Lain did what no one else had ever done: he held simultaneously three world bench records in three different weight classes. A 655-pound bench press weighing 242 pounds. A 700-pound bench press weighing 275 pounds. And a 722-pound bench press in the super heavyweight division. This guy knows what he's talking about.

Think about that: 700 pounds. If you can bench press 250 or 300 pounds right now, you'd need to put another 400 to 450 pounds on the bar just to get into Ken Lain's league.

Yet Ken wasn't some genetically gifted athlete who was just naturally strong at the bench press. He was very smart and knew how to train his body, and what he did can help you in your own training. He used a 10-week bench press power increase program with one heavy day of training and one light day (80 percent of the heavy-day weights), four days a week (Monday/Tuesday/Thursday/Friday).

Along with that, Ken had some tried-and-true techniques that helped him increase his bench, such as the following:

- He liked using a wider grip because the bar had a shorter distance to move. This allowed him to really increase the poundages.
- He used an arc motion when benching. He would lower the weight down to his lower chest and then push the barbell back up so that the weight moved *upward* and *behind* him. When he was finished, the barbell was above his face at about mouth level (see Figure 16.1).
- He believed that breathing was very important. Before he started the bench press, he'd breathe in slightly, and as the bar was being lowered to his chest he'd take another big

breath until his lungs were filled. Once the bar touched his chest, he'd push it off his chest and exhale as he pushed it back up to the starting position.
- He used his lat muscles to help him bench by keeping the elbows as close as possible to his upper body during the movement. At the bottom of the movement, he would bring out his lats, which gave the bar enough momentum to lift off the bottom as the arms, chest, and delts then pushed the weight back up to completion (see Figure 16.2).
- He said it's important to *always* stay tight on the bench and not move your glutes and body once you're set.
- He preferred to use a *slight* arch in his back that would allow him to bring the hips and delts closer together. The arch should be small enough to allow only a few fingers to slide in between the lower back and the bench.
- Unlike many bodybuilders who bench, Ken didn't cheat by using a huge arch that lifted his glutes off the bench. His upper body and

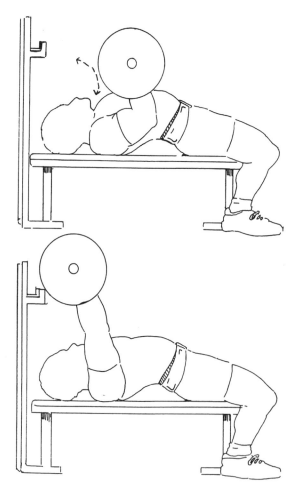

FIGURE 16.1 The arc movement of the bar. Bring the bar down to your chest, just below the nipple line. Then, when pressing the weight, push both upward and backward so that the bar will be positioned above either your chin or nose at lockout.

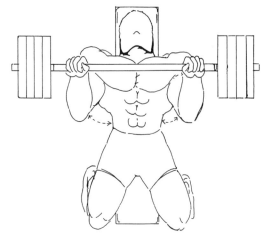

FIGURE 16.2 Avoid flaring out the elbows during the bench press movement. Try to keep your elbows as close to your body as possible in order to allow your powerful back muscles to contribute to the lift.

glutes *always* stayed in contact with the bench and he used his legs, chest, delts, and triceps to help propel the barbell back up (see Figure 16.3).

- He used explosive reps when he pushed the weight up. He said he always used a controlled movement on the way down, and then boom! With all the power he had, he'd drive the weight back up.

ADD 50 POUNDS (OR MORE) TO YOUR BENCH IN 10 WEEKS

All the great bench pressers I've met have training programs they use to reach the bench press stratosphere. Privately, many told me they've used Ken Lain's training tips with great results. Here's one of the best they've used. Based on what Ken told me, the following is an example of a program for anyone who has a 275-pound maximum 1-rep bench press and wants to increase it to 325 pounds at the end of 10 weeks. Your poundages will most likely be different, but simply plug in your current maximum 1-rep bench press weight, add 50 pounds for one new 10-week 1-rep maximum, and calculate the percentages for each workout accordingly. Note: I've rounded off some of the figures by a few pounds in either direction to make

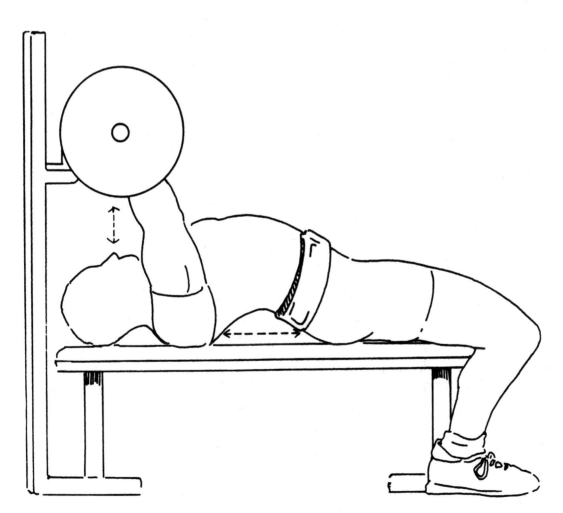

FIGURE 16.3 To reach the degree of tightness required to explode through a single-rep max, you should develop a natural arch in your lower back during the movement.

it easy for you to find the correct barbell plates to use that weight.

Along with doing the bench press, you'll also be doing exercises that will help strengthen your weakest muscle groups and all bodyparts. Your Monday and Thursday workouts will be your *push days*, when you'll train shoulders and triceps. Tuesday and Friday workouts will be your *pull days*, when you'll train back and biceps. Note that on the heavy days you should do a light warm-up. On your light workout days, you should do your regular warm-up.

You'll train legs only once per week, either on a heavy pull day or between regular training days (on a Wednesday, for example). For assistance training, you must follow the percentages given each week and not do more or less than the percentages tell you. For bigger bodyparts, you'll do 12 sets of assistance exercises; for smaller bodyparts, 9 sets.

Believe it or not, Ken also uses other non–bench press exercises that actually help his bench press. You are only as strong as your weakest link, and in this case, it's your weakest muscle group. The chest may be much stronger in comparison to the shoulders and triceps, yet it's the shoulders and triceps that will keep your poundages static unless you specifically train them for the bench. Following are those specific exercises he uses.

Monday (Heavy) and Thursday (Light) Assistance Exercises
Flat bench dumbbell flye: 4 sets of 10 reps

Weighted dip: 4 sets of 8–10 reps

Military press: 4 sets of 8–10 reps

Front lateral raise: 4 sets of 8–10 reps

Close-grip bench press: 4 sets of 8–10 reps

Triceps pressdown: 4 sets of 8–10 reps

Tuesday (Heavy) and Friday (Light) Assistance Exercises
Lat pulldown: 4 sets of 10 reps

Chin-up: 4 sets of 10 reps (You can choose which one you'll do, but do either the lat pulldown or chin-ups each Tuesday and Friday workout)

Dumbbell pullover: 4 sets of 8–10 reps

Seated cable row: 4 sets of 8–10 reps

Bent-over barbell row: 4 sets of 8–10 reps (You can choose which one you'll do, but do either the seated cable row or bent-over barbell row each Tuesday and Friday workout)

Barbell curl: 4 sets of 8–10 reps

Dumbbell curl: 4 sets of 8–10 reps

Legs
Squat: 1–2 warm-up sets followed by 3 heavy sets of 5–8 reps

Leg extension: 5 sets of 12 reps

Leg curl: 4 sets of 10 reps

Seated calf raise: 5 sets of 12 reps

On the eighth week of his bench press program Ken stops doing all assistance exercises and focuses his strength and energy solely on the bench press. On the days he doesn't train—Wednesday, Saturday, and Sunday—he minimizes all other physical activity and gives his body plenty of time to rest and recuperate. That also means getting at least seven hours of sleep each night.

THE POWER BENCH PROGRAM

Week 1
Monday (Heavy)
- 2–3 light warm-up sets
- 3 sets of 10 reps with 180 pounds (55% of target maximum weight, 325)
- Heavy-weight assistance exercises

Thursday (Light)
- 2–3 warm-up sets
- 3 sets of 10 reps with 145 pounds (80% of weight used on Monday's workout)

Week 2
Monday (Heavy)
- 2–3 light warm-up sets
- 3 sets of 9 reps with 195 pounds (60% of target maximum weight)

Thursday (Light)
- 2–3 warm-up sets
- 3 sets of 9 reps with 155 pounds (80% of weight used on Monday's workout)

Week 3
Monday (Heavy)
- 2–3 light warm-up sets
- 3 sets of 8 reps with 210 pounds (65% of target maximum weight)

Thursday (Light)
- 2–3 warm-up sets
- 3 sets of 8 reps with 170 pounds (80% of weight used on Monday's workout)

Week 4
Monday (Heavy)
- 2–3 light warm-up sets
- 3 sets of 7 reps with 225 pounds (70% of target maximum weight)

Thursday (Light)
- 2–3 warm-up sets
- 3 sets of 7 reps with 180 pounds (80% of weight used on Monday's workout)

Week 5
Monday (Heavy)
- 2–3 light warm-up sets
- 3 sets of 6 reps with 245 pounds (75% of target maximum weight)

Thursday (Light)
- 2–3 warm-up sets
- 3 sets of 6 reps with 195 pounds (80% of weight used on Monday's workout)

Week 6
Monday (Heavy)
- 2–3 light warm-up sets
- 3 sets of 5 reps with 260 pounds (80% of target maximum weight)

Thursday (Light)
- 2–3 warm-up sets
- 3 sets of 5 reps with 210 pounds (80% of weight used on Monday's workout)

Week 7
Monday (Heavy)
- 2–3 light warm-up sets
- 2 sets of 4 reps with 275 pounds (85% of target maximum weight)

Thursday (Light)
- 2–3 warm-up sets
- 2 sets of 4 reps with 220 pounds (80% of weight used on Monday's workout)

Week 8
Monday (Heavy)
- 2–3 light warm-up sets
- 2 sets of 3 reps with 290 pounds (90% of target maximum weight)

Thursday (Light)
- 2–3 warm-up sets
- 2 sets of 3 reps with 230 pounds (80% of weight used on Monday's workout)

Week 9
Monday (Heavy)
- 2–3 light warm-up sets
- 1 set of 2 reps with 310 pounds (95% of target maximum weight)

Thursday (Light)
- 2–3 warm-up sets
- 1 set of 2 reps with 250 pounds (80% of weight used on Monday's workout)

Week 10: The Day You Bench 325 Pounds
Monday (Heavy)
- 2–3 light warm-up sets
- 1 rep with 275 pounds
- 1 rep with 310 pounds
- 1 rep with 325 pounds

After completing the 10-week program, give your body a week off from training. (Ken told me it took him up to 21 days to recover from an all-out training program and world-record lift, so judge your body accordingly.) Following a rest break from training, do only regular workouts for one month before beginning your next 10-week program.

PART V

Bodybuilding 201's Best Machine, Freeweight, and Bodyweight-Only Exercises

So many machines. So many new names for exercises that magazines make up in order to make it sound like they created them. The truth is, there are no new exercises. Machines still function in the movement plane of the human body and are essentially designed to mimic that and freeweight exercises.

Regardless of how many different things you try or how long you try them, odds are that you'll come back to the basics if you want great results year after year. The smart people always do and always will. These exercises are the foundation builders, and the more foundation you build, the longer that foundation will last: that is, for the rest of your life.

I'm not interested in hype; I want what works now and what will work next year, in 5 years, in 10 years, in 20 years. You bought my book (thank you) because you want that, too, so the best I can do for you is to give you the *Bodybuilding 201* exercise all-stars that have passed the test to make it into the exercise hall of fame. They stand out for one simple reason: they work! Unlike my other books, on many of the following exercises I'm not going to give you a strict number of sets and reps you should perform. As a *Bodybuilding 201* athlete, you have reached the level where you know what kinds of exercises, sets, and reps your body responds well to. On those exercises for which I do suggest sets and reps, try them, but do not hesitate to adjust anything, whenever and wherever you want. Always keep your workouts fun, fresh, and exciting.

These are my favorite and most effective exercises for the *Bodybuilding 201* athlete.

17

The *Bodybuilding 201* Chest Exercises

I think it's best that you focus your chest work on inclines, which are superior to the flat bench press. Many bodybuilders who have done the flat bench press for years have impressive mid- to lower-chest development, but the upper chest always seems to lag behind. But bodybuilders who've done mostly incline work have chests that look big, thick, and complete, from top to bottom. So if you're putting work into getting that chest looking great, why not make your time count and do the exercise that will produce complete results in one movement?

Use the following tips for the barbell incline press.

- Set the incline bench at roughly 25 to 35 degrees, or use a fixed incline bench. The higher the incline, the more the work shifts to the shoulders. Keep the incline high enough that it's not a flat bench, yet low enough to keep the work centered more on the chest and not the delts.
- Keep your glutes firmly in the seat and your upper body and head

against the incline bench. Your feet should be flat on the floor, spread fairly wide for more stability and support.
- Bring the dumbbells up over your face until your arms are fully extended.
- Slowly lower the weights until the weights are lowered to chest level.
- Be sure to keep your elbows at or near shoulder level and pointed behind you. Keeping the elbows at this level seems to make the chest work harder and gives it a good stretch.
- Bring the arms and weights up again until the arms are fully extended, but don't let the dumbbells touch each other at the top. Keep them about 6 to 9 inches apart.

30-Degree Dumbbell Incline Press
I believe this is one of the most effective exercises to build and strengthen your chest. The degree of stretch and movement is incredible if you do it right.

Always make your first set a light warm-up set. Do 1 to 2 sets of 8 to 12

30-degree dumbbell incline press (a)

30-degree dumbbell incline press (b)

reps and really stretch the chest by allowing the dumbbells to come down as low as possible. If you feel like you need it, go ahead and do another warm-up set. You want to get the blood pumping and the delts, pecs, and triceps warmed.

After your warm-up, pick a weight that you can do for 6 to 8 reps. Make sure you lower the weights far enough to get a great chest stretch. Always control the weight; don't do fast reps. Normal-pace, steady reps do the trick. Don't rest between reps; rest no longer than 60 seconds between sets.

Keep your glutes tight against the seat and your back firmly against the back pad. Be sure to bring your elbows straight down toward the floor (not back behind you) and bring the dumbbells down until the weight plates are

even with your chest. You must lower the weights down as far as possible in order to get a good stretch. As you bring the weights back up and over you, be sure that you do not allow the weights to touch each other. At the top of the movement, keep the weights about 6 to 8 inches apart.

Barbell Incline Press
The tips for the dumbbell press apply here, with these exceptions:

- Hold the barbell with a grip slightly wider than shoulder width.
- Be sure to fully extend your arms with the barbell directly over your face. Really squeeze and contract the chest when your arms reach this position.

■ Lower the barbell until it actually touches the top of your chest/lower neck. Make sure the elbows are up high and pointed back as far as possible in order to get a great stretch.

Dumbbell Flye

Pick a weight that you can do for 10 to 12 reps. Don't use a heavy weight. At this point you are interested only in pumping the muscle. Using a slightly inclined flat bench (about 10 to 20 degrees) works well for this exercise. With a dumbbell in each hand, slowly lower the weights out to your sides and away from your body. Your arms should be almost fully extended, slightly bent at the elbows. Really get a good stretch.

As you bring the weights back up to the starting position at the top, do not press the weight like you would if you were doing a dumbbell bench press. Bring the weights up in a big arc or circle—like you're putting your arms around a big barrel—until you reach the top position with the weights above your head.

Dumbbell Incline Flye

Do this exercise just like the regular dumbbell flye, only use a bench you can elevate to about 25 to 40 degrees. Get a nice, deep stretch at the bottom of the movement; bring the weights up in a semicircle and don't let them touch each other at the top of the movement. Keep them about 6 to 8

Barbell incline press (a)

Barbell incline press (b)

Dumbbell flye (a)

Dumbbell flye (b)

Dumbbell incline flye (a)

Dumbbell incline flye (b)

inches apart so you'll keep a good contraction on the pecs.

Wide-Arm Push-Up with Feet Elevated
This can be a great chest exercise if done correctly. You'll use only your bodyweight.

Place your feet on a flat surface that's elevated about 1 to 2 feet off the ground (as shown in the photo). Only your feet, not any part of your legs, should be touching the bench. Place your palms flat on the floor, fingers facing forward. Keep your arms and

hands at shoulder level spread about a foot wider than shoulder width. While keeping your upper body in a straight line with your legs, bend the elbows so that your body lowers until it's about 1 to 2 inches away from touching the floor. Hold this position for 1 to 2 seconds, then bring the body up by extending the arms until they are locked. Squeeze and contract the chest at the top and hold the contraction for 1 to 2 seconds. Repeat. Do 10 to 12 reps or as many as you are able to complete.

Wide-arm push-up with feet elevated (a)

Wide-arm push-up with feet elevated (b)

Close-Hand Push-Up with Feet Elevated

Place your hands together (one on top of the other) and position them just under the lower-chest area. Place your feet on an elevated flat bench behind you. The higher your feet are off the ground, the more resistance in the exercise and the harder the movement will be. Lower your body until it rests on top of your hands, then press up and lock your elbows. Go for as many reps as possible.

Dumbbell Flat Bench Press/ Flye Combination

You'll be doing two slightly different chest exercises here. Pick a weight that you can lift for 9 to 12 reps. Lie on the flat bench with your upper body completely on the bench with either your feet on the floor or your knees bent and legs off the floor, elevated above the flat bench.

With palms forward and arms and weights locked above your head, slowly lower the weights down and out to your sides until your arms are in a straight line with your shoulders. Your elbows should point down and a bit below the top of the flat bench. That's when you know you're getting into big stretch territory. You should feel it in the chest. Go as far down as you com-

Close-hand push-up with feet elevated (a)

Close-hand push-up with feet elevated (b)

Dumbbell flat bench press/flye combination (a)

Dumbbell flat bench press/flye combination (b)

fortably can. Press the weights back up to the top and repeat for a total of 8 reps.

After the eighth rep, turn your hands so that your palms are now facing each other and not forward. It's now time for flyes. Bring the arms down like you did with the press, only this time, think of the movement like putting your arms around a big, wide barrel. Get a deep stretch at the bottom, and as you bring the weights up in a semicircle, don't let them touch each other at the top of the movement. Keep them about 6 to 8 inches apart so you'll keep a good contraction on the pecs. Do 8 reps.

Standing Cable Crunch

This exercise is much like a flye, only you're doing the movement standing between two cable weight stacks. You'll be using a high pulley with a stirrup-

style handle connected to left and right weight stacks. The keys to getting the most from it are the stretch (when the arms and cable handles are out to your sides) and the contraction (when the hands and cable handles are close together in front of your body).

Stand between two weight stacks, equidistant from each so you'll get an equal pull from the left and right cables. While holding the handles in each hand, let your arms fully extend out to your sides so that you get a good stretch in your chest. Keep your legs about shoulder-width apart and put either your left or right foot slightly in front of your body.

Bend your upper body forward slightly. Bring the cable handles together in front of you by bending your elbows and bringing your arms and hands together in front of you. As your hands are coming in front of

Standing cable crunch (a)

you, squeeze and contract the pecs together until they reach the point where you feel the greatest contraction. This will be your stopping point. Hold the hands in that contracted position for a count or two, then let the arms return back out to your sides until they are fully extended. This will be your beginning point.

Standing cable crunch (b)

18

The *Bodybuilding 201* Back and Traps Exercises

Now that you've got the chest pumped up, let's keep things "upper body," as we move to exercises for the back and traps.

Barbell Shrugs with Static Holds

Have you ever seen a powerful-looking physique that didn't have big traps? Of course not. Anyone who has great traps does deadlifts and shrugs. I'm about to show you a way to do shrugs that will pack slabs of muscle on those traps.

The best place to do shrugs is in a power rack. If you can use a power rack, great. If not, then do regular shrugs with a barbell on the floor. If you are using a rack, set the rack bar so the barbell rests at knee level. This will be the starting position.

After a 1- to 2-set warm-up with a lighter weight, load the barbell with a weight that you can do for a tough 10 reps. Don't make it too heavy, but don't make it too light, either. Take a shoulder-width grip on the barbell. You can use both hands in an overhand grip or a combination of one hand over and the other hand under.

Barbell shrugs with static holds (a)

Barbell shrugs with static holds (b)

Keeping your legs slightly bent, upper body erect, and arms locked, raise your shoulders straight up toward the ceiling. Don't row your shoulders forward and backward; just raise them straight up and down. At the top of the movement, hold the barbell for 1 to 2 seconds, then slowly lower it back to the starting position. Do your set, rest 30 to 60 seconds, then do another set.

Depending on how many sets you do, on your last one or two sets, try something a bit different on the final reps. Instead of lowering the barbell all the way down and then shrugging it straight up, set the barbell down and shrug your shoulders all the way up, then grab the barbell and hold it at the top position, then slowly lower it.

T-Bar or Dumbbell Row

T-bar rows did more for building and widening my back than any other exercise. You might find they'll do the same for you. There are two ways to do them.

The first way is with a T-bar. Load a T-bar with enough weight that you can do 5 to 8 reps. Place your feet close to the T-handle. Once you grab the handle with an overhand close grip (hands about 6 to 8 inches apart), your hands will be only a few inches in front of the tops of your feet. Keep your knees slightly bent and keep your upper body at a 90-degree angle to the floor. Maintain this position throughout the exercise; use only your arms to pull the weight up and down.

Bend your knees until your upper body is bent forward over the weight plates and it reaches a near flat position parallel to the floor. With your legs and upper body locked in position, bring the weight up to your chest by bringing the arms and elbows back behind you. Let the weight touch your chest, then lower it all the way down

T-bar row with plate-loaded machine (a)

T-bar row with plate-loaded machine (b)

Dumbbell row (a)

Dumbbell row (b)

until the arms are fully straight and locked out. Really feel the lats stretch.

Do not round your back at the bottom of the exercise. Even when the arms and weight are at the lowest point of the rep, keep the back flat and parallel to the floor.

The other way I recommend performing the T-bar row is with a plate-loaded machine (as illustrated in the photo). Keep your feet and upper body stationary while performing the exer-

cise. Moving only the arms, bring the weight up as far as possible, then lower until the arms are fully extended.

I prefer T-bar rows, but if you can't do them, then dumbbell rows will do. Work just one arm at a time. Keep the leg on the floor of the side that you are working (for example, left leg/left arm). Place the hand that's not holding the dumbbell on the flat bench to support the upper body.

Keep your upper body at a 45- to 60-degree angle from start to finish. The only muscle you should move is the arm that is rowing the weight up and down. Keep your head and neck in line with your upper body and looking forward.

To begin, let your arm fully straighten and allow the dumbbell to come all the way down (it should be close to the floor). While keeping your body in the locked position, bring the arm up and elbow back, drawing the weight up so that the dumbbell touches the side of your upper body near the waist. Squeeze and contract the lats at the top, then slowly lower the arm and weight back down as far as possible. Get a good stretch in the bottom position. Do the same number of reps for each side.

Chin-Up or Wide-Grip Machine Pulldown

To execute the chin-up, go to the chinning bar and place your hands about 8 to 10 inches wider than shoulder-width apart. Pull yourself all the way up until your chin is above the bar. As you pull yourself up, you may slightly arch your back and allow your chest to come forward. After you reach the top, slowly lower yourself until your arms are fully extended. Keep your upper body straight and your legs bent with your feet behind you. Repeat. Do as many reps as possible. Rest no longer than 35 to 45 seconds between sets.

Wide-grip machine pulldown (a)

Wide-grip machine pulldown (b)

For the pulldown, keep the upper body erect but with a slight arch to the back. Bring the bar down until it touches your upper chest, just below the neck. Be sure to bring the elbows down and behind you to give your back muscles a more intense contraction. Allow the bar to slowly return above you until your arms are fully extended.

Reverse-Grip EZ-Bar or Barbell Row

Load an EZ-bar or barbell with the most weight you can lift for 6 reps. (You'll likely find the EZ-bar easier to use than a barbell, but either is fine.) Keep your knees bent slightly and your upper torso bent forward at roughly a 60- to 80-degree angle. Using a reverse grip (underhand), pull the weight up and into your waist/lower abs. Be sure

to bring your elbows back behind you as far as possible in order to really contract your back muscles.

Low-Pulley Cable Bar Row

This movement is the same as the reverse-grip EZ-bar or barbell row. The differences: you'll stand on a flat bench or platform rather than on the floor, and you'll use a straight or curved bar connected to a low pulley on a machine. You can do these without standing on a bench, but you'll get a much better stretch and a greater range of movement with the bench or platform.

Reverse-Grip Straight-Bar Lat Machine Pulldown

Use the same body position that you'd use for regular pulldowns with an over-

Reverse-grip EZ-bar or barbell row (a)

Reverse-grip EZ-bar or barbell row (b)

Low-pulley cable bar row (a)

Low-pulley cable bar row (b)

Reverse-grip straight-bar lat machine pulldown (a)

Reverse-grip straight-bar lat machine pulldown (b)

hand grip, but use an underhand grip instead (palms facing your body instead of away from your body) and keep your hands about 6 to 10 inches apart. Be sure to bring the bar down to your lower chest and keep your elbows straight back behind you so you can get a good back contraction. Allow the weight to come all the way up until your arms are fully extended above your head. Really go for the lat stretch.

One-Arm Low-Pulley Cable Row

You can do two different exercises in one simply by changing your hand position during the movement. Take a stirrup-style handle attached to a low pulley. Load a weight heavy enough so that you can do 11 to 14 reps. With your left side facing the weight stack, grab the handle with your right hand so that your palm is facing the floor and your right arm is fully extended in front of you.

Bend your knees and your upper body, then pull your arm back behind you. As you pull, turn your hand so that your palm faces upward by the time your arm comes all the way back and your hand reaches your side. Remember, your palm faces down at the beginning and up at the end. Let the arm return to the starting position and repeat for 11 to 14 reps. Repeat on your other side for 11 to 14 reps.

Hyperextension

On a hyperextension bench, position your upper body so it doesn't touch the bench; it should be able to move freely. With your arms in front of you tucked near your chest, bend your upper torso until your head is near the floor. Hold this position for 1 to 2 seconds. Then slowly raise your upper torso until it is even and in a direct line with your legs. Do not hyperextend your upper body by raising it higher than your legs. After you've

One-arm low-pulley cable row (a)

One-arm low-pulley cable row (b)

Hyperextension (a)

Hyperextension (b)

done 12 to 15 reps, immediately turn over onto your back and do hyper-bench crunch/sit-ups to complete the front-to-back lower back/ab set.

Chin-Up

Over the years, chins have helped many bodybuilders widen out. As eight-time Mr. Olympia Lee Haney once told me, "It's one thing to do a lat pulldown, but there's nothing like pulling your whole body up and down like a chin-up." Absolutely. Chins can be tough, but they produce great results. Just hang in there if you're not able to do a bunch of reps right away. They'll come. And if you ever wonder whether chins are really that good, just remember that the Navy SEALS, Special Operations Forces, and

Chin-up with wide grip (a)

Chin-up with narrow grip (b)

other military units train and test their soldiers on chin-ups, not lat pulldowns.

Take a wider than shoulder-width overhand grip on a chin bar as illustrated in photo (a). Or you can use a narrower underhand grip, as illustrated in photo (b). Bend your knees and raise your calves and feet so they are behind your body. Pull yourself up until your chin is at or near the chin bar. Go higher, to upper-chest level, if you can. As you reach the top, concentrate on keeping your elbows back behind you. This will help give you a better lat contraction. Slowly lower your body until the arms are fully extended and you feel a great lat stretch.

Do as many reps as you can. Once you can no longer do full-range reps, do a few short-range reps each set. If

you can do only 2 or 3 full-range reps and the rest short-range reps, then do them. The only way to get your body stronger and accustomed to the movement is simply to do it. It may not look pretty, but you'll be getting stronger very quickly.

Wide-Grip Barbell Upright Row
This is a trap/upper-back exercise that also works the side deltoid.

Take a very wide overhand grip on a barbell. Your hands should almost touch the inside of the closest weight plates. Keep your body erect. Lower the barbell all the way down in front of you. Instead of allowing it to rest against your body at the starting position, move the barbell away from and in front of your body about 4 to 6 inches. Once you do that, you'll immediately feel the delts working. Keeping

Wide-grip barbell upright row (a)

Wide-grip barbell upright row (b)

the bar always about 4 to 6 inches away from the body, raise the arms up and elbows high, bringing the barbell up until it reaches chin level. Hold it there for 1 to 2 seconds, then slowly lower it. Don't let the bar come closer than 4 to 6 inches from your body during the entire exercise.

Seated Cable Row

Sitting at the cable row machine, grab a stirrup-style bar so that both palms face each other. Keep a slight bend in your knees and hold your upper torso erect. Pull your elbows back behind you and the bar down low and back until it hits your lower stomach. Lower the weight, fully extend your arms in front of you, and allow your upper torso to come only slightly forward for a good lat stretch.

Straight-Bar Pulldown/Pullover

This is like a combination exercise. As you pull the bar down in front of you for the first part of the exercise, it feels

like a pulldown, and as the bar comes up, over your head, and stretches the lats at the top of the movement, it feels like a pullover. You won't need heavy weights for this, nor will you be able to use them.

Use a straight bar connected to a high pulley on the lat machine. With an overhand grip, place your hands on the straight bar so that they are slightly wider than shoulder-width apart. Keep your legs together and locked and let your upper torso bend forward slightly.

Keeping your arms locked from start to finish, bring the arms and the bar down in front of you until the bar almost touches the top of your upper thighs/waist. Slowly let the arms and bar come back up, and as you do, bend the upper body a few more inches forward as your arms and the bar come up and over you. Really feel the lat stretch as the arms/bar are returning to the top starting position.

Seated cable row (a)

Seated cable row (b)

Straight-bar pulldown/pullover (a)

Straight-bar pulldown/pullover (b)

19

The *Bodybuilding 201* Shoulders and Delts Exercises

From back and traps we move to shoulders and delts, where the emphasis is on specific form and burns.

One-Arm Standing Dumbbell Press
A super mass builder, this movement is very similar to the regular dumbbell press, except you work only one arm at

One-arm standing dumbbell press (a)

One-arm standing dumbbell press (b)

a time instead of two. You may not be able to use as much weight as you could if you were using two dumbbells, but this exercise will make you really focus on the delt being worked instead of having to split that focus on two of them at the same time.

Be sure to keep your upper body in a fixed position from start to finish. The arm that's moving the weight up and down should be the only bodypart that moves. Don't cheat by bending your legs up and down or lowering the side of the body of the delt you are working.

After a good warm-up set or two, pick a weight that will allow you to do 5 to 7 reps. I prefer doing this exercise standing with a weight in one hand and my other hand holding on to the top of a bench for support.

Using an overhand grip, bring the dumbbell all the way up above your head and fully extend your arm. Bring the weight back down and lower it until the side of the dumbbell is at shoulder level. Always go for the full extension at the top and full stretch at the bottom.

Dumbbell Side Lateral

The trick to making the delts work hard is not using heavy weights but keeping the delts moving with little rest between reps and sets. You want to make them burn!

Take a pair of dumbbells and either sit on a flat bench or stand. Allow the weights to come down to your side, but don't let them touch your body. Keep them about 6 to 10 inches away from your body. This is the starting position.

Raise the weights up and directly out to your sides. Keep the weights in a direct line with your upper body. Bring the weights up only as high as your shoulders and hold them there for 1 to 2 seconds. Slowly lower the weights back down and repeat.

Standing dumbbell side lateral (a)

Standing dumbbell side lateral (b)

Seated dumbbell side lateral (a)

Seated dumbbell side lateral (b)

Seated dumbbell side lateral (side view)

Bent-Over Opposing-Grip Cable Lateral

Think of this as a dumbbell bent-over lateral, only this time you'll be using a cable, with one hand at a time. Start with the upper torso bent over at 90 degrees. As you continue to do the

Bent-over opposing-grip cable lateral

reps, start elevating your upper torso until it is in a near-vertical position. You'll feel this exercise all over your delts.

Barbell Front Press

In a standing position, grip a barbell wider than shoulder width. Start with the barbell resting on the front deltoids. Press the weight straight up and over your head until your arms are fully locked. Lower the weight to the starting position and repeat. For a real burner, try stopping the weight about halfway through the movement, then press it up about 3 or 4 inches and do this for about 10 quick repetitions.

Seated Dumbbell Press

There's just no better way to put big, thick, wide delts on a physique than heavy presses. One of the most effective presses for this purpose is the seated dumbbell press. Compared to barbells, dumbbells allow for a freer movement and a slightly greater range of motion that can make all the difference between feeling it a little or a lot.

Use an incline bench that you can fully elevate so that the back pad is straight up and down at almost 90 degrees. I like just a very slight incline

Barbell front press (a)

Barbell front press (b)

Seated dumbbell press (a)

Seated dumbbell press (b)

from vertical (perhaps one notch back) because it gives me a bit more freedom to find the most comfortable exercise groove to do the presses.

With your body snugly against the seat and back pad and a dumbbell in each hand, bring the dumbbells up until they reach shoulder level, then press them up and directly over your head. Don't clang the dumbbells together at the top. Keep them about 4 to 6 inches apart.

Lower the weights, and as you do so, keep the arms in a straight line with the upper body and the elbows pointing straight down. Bring the weights down until they reach shoulder level, then press them up again. Some people will get great results by locking the elbows at the top. Others feel it more by pressing the weights up to near lockout. Find out which of the two works better for you.

20

The *Bodybuilding 201* Triceps Exercises

With the triceps being responsible for about two-thirds of your arm size (not to mention all that strength), it's time we got serious about making your triceps the best they can be.

Seated Dumbbell French Press

This exercise will really pack size and strength on your triceps. The key to really feeling this exercise is to make sure the elbows are fully warmed up. Don't use the heavy iron until those elbows and triceps tendons have been warmed up with 2 to 3 sets of 15 to 20 reps of triceps pressdowns or push-ups and 1 or 2 sets of light (40 to 50 percent of your max weight) seated dumbbell behind-the-head French presses. You must take a few extra minutes to do this in order to avoid injury and get the most from this exercise.

Once you feel your triceps are ready, pick a dumbbell that you can lift for 10 reps but that will require you to push yourself a bit on the eighth or ninth rep. Sit on a bench, preferably one with a small back support. The smaller benches used for doing presses

or curls work great. Be sure the back support will allow you to lower the dumbbell all the way down behind your head without the dumbbell hit-

Seated dumbbell French press (a)

Seated dumbbell French press (b)

while you keep your upper arm close to your head, as this will stretch your triceps. Stretch each arm for 10 to 20 seconds.

Lying EZ-Bar French Press Away from Head

This is another great triceps movement, but arm position is crucial to make it really work. Lie down on your back on a flat bench. Place your head at the very end of one side of the bench, but keep the head and neck on the bench. Raise an EZ-bar overhead, bringing your upper arms down and close to your head. Bring your arms and the weight behind your head. Your upper arms should be at about a 45-degree angle behind your head. Keeping your upper arms in this position during the entire exercise, bend the elbows and lower the weight down and behind your head. (Don't do what people call skullcrushers, lowering the weight right above your face.) Get a great triceps stretch.

ting the back support and stopping you from doing a full range of movement.

Grasp the dumbbell with both hands so that your hands are clasped together and your palms are turned up, facing the ceiling. While keeping your upper arms close to your head, raise the dumbbell above your head and slowly lower the weight all the way down behind your head until your triceps are fully stretched. Raise the dumbbell back up over your head until your arms are completely locked. Squeeze your triceps hard for an intense contraction. Slowly lower the weight. Repeat until you've done 10 reps. Rest no longer than 45 to 60 seconds and repeat the set, for a total of 2 sets.

Once you've finished, raise your arm above your head and allow your forearm to come back behind you

Lying EZ-bar French press away from head (a)

Lying EZ-bar French press away from head (b)

Bring your hands, forearms, and the weight up until your arms are fully locked and the triceps are fully contracted. As you're bringing the weight down, allow your upper arms to move down toward the floor behind you and below your head. Keep the upper arms there as you extend your hands up and lock your elbows.

Machine Pressdown with Straight Bar

Use a moderate weight on your first set, then increase the weight on each of the next three sets. This will ensure that your triceps tendon is fully warmed once you hit the heaviest weight.

Place your hands about 8 to 10 inches apart on the straight bar. Lock your upper arms and elbows close to your sides and move only the lower arms and elbows as you do the exercise. Allow the bar to come no higher than chest level, and be sure to fully extend the arms and contract the triceps hard as you press the weight

Machine pressdown with straight bar (a)

Machine pressdown with straight bar (b)

Reverse-grip pressdown with straight bar (a)

down. Rest no longer than 45 seconds between sets. Increase the weight for each exercise by at least 10 percent each set.

Reverse-Grip Pressdown with Straight Bar

This change-of-pace triceps finishing exercise is easy to do: take a straight bar and do pressdowns like you'd normally do them, but use an underhand grip. Go for higher reps (20 or more).

Dumbbell Kickback

The kickback is a great triceps movement. You can work both arms at once or one arm at a time. With your knees bent slightly, one resting on a flat bench, bend your upper torso 70 to 90 degrees. Keep the arm you are working locked tight into your side and make sure your elbow is raised higher than your back. Extend the arm with the dumbbell up and behind you until the

Reverse-grip pressdown with straight bar (b)

Dumbbell kickback (a)

Dumbbell kickback (b)

elbow is locked. Hold in the contracted position for a second or two, then slowly return to the starting position.

Close-Grip Bench Press

This is simply the standard bench press with different hand and elbow positions. Place your hands toward the center of the barbell about 6 to 10 inches apart. Bring the barbell down to mid-chest level. The bar will touch your chest at the bottom of the exercise. Keep your elbows tight and close to your lats as you do each rep. This will help give you more power and stability, and it's the way a lot of great powerlifters do their heavy bench presses. Be sure to lock your arms completely once the weight is overhead. Feel the big triceps contraction. Once you can no longer do full-range reps, do a few short-range reps (only a few inches down, then up).

Bent-Over High-Pulley Cable Rope Extension

Begin this exercise as if you were getting ready to do a normal machine pressdown, but use a V-shaped rope instead of a bar. Once you've selected the weight and grabbed each end of the rope, turn your body around so that you face away from the weight stack. Keep the legs together with knees slightly bent. One leg can be a few inches in front of the other and the body. Keep your arms above your head as you hold the rope.

Bend your upper body forward so that it's at a 30- to 60-degree angle. Bring your upper arms close to your head and keep them there from start to finish. Extend the hands forward and lock the elbows so that your triceps are fully contracted. Hold the arms and rope in this position for a count or two and then slowly let the

Close-grip bench press (a)

Close-grip bench press (b)

forearms, hands, and rope come back and up over your head until the triceps are fully stretched. Repeat this sequence until finished with your set.

Dip

Dips and dumbbell French presses are the two best mass- and power-building exercises for triceps. These two movements are like squats for the back of your arms and will do more to add pounds to your bench press and shoulder press than you may have imagined possible.

The V-shaped dip bar works great because it allows you to isolate other muscles better than the even-spaced dip bars. Doing dips with hands closer together, at the narrowest part of the V, will hit the triceps more. Doing dips with hands farther apart, at the widest part of the V, will hit the chest more. Your elbow position—either in and

close to your upper body or out and away from your body—will also vary the way the movement feels.

Your legs may remain straight up and down and in line with your upper body, provided your dip bar is high enough off the floor that your body has room to come all the way down (with legs straight) when you reach the bottom of the dip. Or you may bend your knees and keep your lower legs and feet behind your body, perhaps crossing your ankles.

Dips can be tough on the shoulders and chest, so make sure you're really warmed up before doing them. Consider how far you want to come down. You might like to try one set coming all the way down as far as comfortably possible. On another set, try coming only halfway down. On another set, do partial reps by allowing a slight bend at the elbows and lower-

Bent-over high-pulley cable rope extension (a)

Bent-over high-pulley cable rope extension (b)

Dip (a)

Dip (b)

ing the upper body just a few inches. Best of all, mix it up; try doing a set in which you do the first few reps all the way down, the next few reps halfway down, and the final reps with quick partial reps of only a few inches.

Start out by doing these with just your bodyweight. Once it gets easy to

do 12 to 15 reps with your bodyweight, start adding weight by using a dipping belt and chain (to hold weight plates or a dumbbell between your legs).

21

The *Bodybuilding 201* Biceps Exercises

OK, OK. I know biceps are *the* muscles you want to look great, so relax. Here are some killer exercises.

Seated Partial Dumbbell Curl

This is a terrific exercise for the biceps.

Use a flat bench or a mini-seat with a small back pad that you'd use when doing shoulder presses. After a good 1- or 2-set warm-up of 8 to 12 reps, pick a weight that you can curl—with both arms at the same time—for 7 to 8 reps with moderate effort, but that will have you really pushing it if you go for 9 or 10 reps. Once you've picked that weight, use it for all 10 sets of 10 reps.

While seated on the bench and keeping your upper body erect, bring your arms straight down to your sides. Your palms should face straight out in front of you and straight up toward the ceiling as you curl the weight up.

Begin curling the weight up, stopping the dumbbells about three-quarters of the way up, or at shoulder level. Find the position where your biceps are peak contracted. Once you reach this position, slowly bring your elbows straight up and out in front of you for an even greater contraction. Hold for a second; then, while keeping your arms in this position, slowly lower the weight until your arms are fully extended.

As your arms come close to reaching the fully extended position, slowly lower your upper arms down and back to your side until they reach the starting position. Allow only a 1-second peak contraction rest between reps. Do not rest any longer than 45 seconds between sets.

If you do these the way I've described, you will feel the most intense burn you have ever felt! The key to making the biceps grow and get stronger is to peak contract and not allow the muscle to rest very long before you hit it again. Remember, make the muscle work harder by creating intensity in every exercise and workout.

Thumbs-Up Dumbbell Curl

Here's a great biceps workout that will pump your arms up like a balloon. It works the brachialis (the muscle under-

Seated partial dumbbell curl (a)

Seated partial dumbbell curl (b)

Thumbs-up dumbbell curl (a)

Thumbs-up dumbbell curl (b)

neath the ball or peak of the biceps that you see when you flex your arm) and biceps at the same time.

Sit at the end of a flat bench and keep your upper torso erect. Hold dumbbells in each hand, keeping your thumbs up and palms facing each other. Curl the weights up, and as the dumbbells get closer to your shoulders start turning the wrists so that your thumbs finish turned out and away from your body. Contract your biceps hard at the top of the movement and hold for 1 to 2 seconds before lowering the weights. As you lower the weights, turn your wrist again so that your thumbs face up and your palms face each other.

Seated Incline Dumbbell Curl

Arm position affects where and how much you'll feel this movement. Adjust the bench so that it's set at a 30- to 45-degree angle. Keep the upper body securely positioned throughout the

exercise and allow the shoulders to come just slightly forward, if at all. After you've done a light warm-up set of standing dumbbell curls, pick a weight heavy enough that you can do only 6 to 8 reps.

Keep the elbows pulled in close to the sides of the bench and turn the arms slightly outward and away from the body. Be sure to allow the weights to come all the way down so the arms are fully locked and all the way up until the biceps reach full contraction.

Keep your back and head against the back pad and your glutes planted firmly on the seat. Let your arms hang down at your sides. With your thumbs up and your palms facing each other, curl the weight up, and as you do, turn your wrists until your palms face upward. Be sure to keep your elbows in one position and close to the bench throughout the exercise.

Bring the weights up until they are at shoulder level. You must find the

Seated incline dumbbell curl (a)

Seated incline dumbbell curl (b)

place at the top of the curl where you feel the greatest biceps contraction. Each person is different, so really concentrate and find the right spot for you. Slowly lower the weight until the arms are fully extended. Continue until you've done 6 to 8 reps.

Barbell Preacher Curl

Barbell preacher curls will work the lower biceps and give you lots of fullness there. Do these on the side of the bench that has a slight angle (not the 90-degree steep side). Take a barbell that's light enough that you can do 18 to 22 reps. Because you're doing high reps, don't worry about using heavy weights.

Take a shoulder-width grip on a barbell and place your elbows on the bench so that they are only 8 to 10 inches apart. Remember that your elbows must be narrower than your grip, so keep hands out and elbows in. Lower the weight until your arms are fully extended. Don't hyperextend the

Barbell preacher curl (a)

Barbell preacher curl (b)

elbows by lowering the weight so quickly that it injures your tendons and elbows. Slow and steady is the key.

Once the arms are fully extended, slowly curl the weight up until your biceps are fully contracted. Do not allow the weight to come up to the top and then fall back toward your shoulders. If that happens, you've gone too far and you've passed the point of maximal biceps contraction.

Reverse-Grip EZ-Bar Row Curl

This exercise employs an EZ-bar because it takes the strain off the biceps and is much more comfortable than a straight bar. Grab an EZ-bar with a reverse (underhand) grip and bend your upper body 60 to 80 degrees.

Keeping your head up and looking forward, bring the weight up and into your waist. Your elbows should point behind you. In this position, really contract the lats. The farther back you can bring your elbows behind you, the more you'll be able to feel it in your back/lat muscles. Lower the bar and repeat.

Bent-Over Barbell Concentration Curl

This exercise will really get the blood flowing in the arms, especially after 3 sets of reverse-grip EZ-bar row curls. With a grip that's about shoulder width, take a barbell and bend your torso until it's about 90 degrees, or parallel to the floor. Keep your legs straight but with a slight bend in the knees.

While holding the barbell, let your arms hang down until they are completely straight. Keeping your upper arms in that position, curl the weight up until your biceps are fully contracted. Don't allow the weight to come back toward you any farther than that. You want to keep the biceps stretched at the bottom and contracted at the top. Do 20 to 30 nonstop reps

Reverse-grip EZ-bar row curl (a)

Reverse-grip EZ-bar row curl (b)

Bent-over barbell concentration curl (a)

Bent-over barbell concentration curl (b)

per set. Allow no more than 20 seconds of rest between sets.

Standing EZ-Bar Curl

You'll find that you can curl a heck of a lot more weight with an EZ-bar than a regular barbell. It takes the stress off the wrists by allowing a more comfortable position for your hands, and it feels a bit different because your hands are closer together, closer to the center of the body.

Keep your upper body erect and your legs straight (if you must bend your knees, bend only very slightly). Keep your elbows and upper arms tucked close to your sides from start to finish. Take a fairly close grip on the bar. Your palms will be facing upward, slightly turned toward each other.

Curl the weight up until you feel your biceps fully contract. Going back any farther toward the front delts will take the stress off the biceps. Lower the weight until the arms are fully locked and the weight is touching your thighs.

Thumbs-Up Cable Curl with Rope

For hitting the brachialis, this exercise is tough to beat. Most bodybuilders want big biceps but don't do much to work the brachialis. But if they would, those arms would grow. (Think of the brachialis as the foundation the biceps sit on.) You can use a V-bar for this exercise if you can't find a rope, but the rope works better.

Stand about 12 to 18 inches away from a low-pulley machine. Grab hold of each end of the rope that's connected to the low pulley. While keeping your elbows and upper arms close to your sides and your thumbs up, curl the rope up until you reach full contraction of the biceps. Keep the thumbs in the up position from start to finish. Always lower the weight until the arms are locked and fully extended below you. Nonstop reps work great with this exercise.

Standing EZ-bar curl (a)

Standing EZ-bar curl (b)

Thumbs-up cable curl with rope (a)

Thumbs-up cable curl with rope (b)

22

The *Bodybuilding 201* Forearms Exercises

Forearms get worked in nearly every upper-body exercise you do, and lots of people get enough forearm work without any additional forearm workout. However, if you'd like to pack a little more size and power on them, read on.

Seated Barbell Roll-Off and Roll-Up

Lots of different forearm exercises are available, but this is one of the best. To really feel it, you need to position your body just right.

Choose a barbell with a thinner bar, such as a chrome barbell. Try to stay away from a regular-width Olympic or powerlifter barbell. You want the barbell to roll off your fingers. With a barbell in your hands, sit down on a flat bench.

Keep your forearms and elbows on the flat bench at all times. Never allow them to come up off the bench. Be sure that only your wrists and hands are hanging off the end of the bench. Squeeze your legs together so they are bracing your forearms on the bench.

With the barbell in your hands, slowly open your hands and let the

Seated barbell roll-off and roll-up (a)

Seated barbell roll-off and roll-up (b)

barbell roll down until it reaches the ends of your fingers. Then slowly roll the barbell back up into your palms and close your hands as you bring them as far as you can toward your forearms. Hold the barbell in this fully contracted position for 2 to 3 seconds, then slowly lower it again and repeat.

After you've done your last rep and last set, place the palms of your hands against a wall and raise your arms higher than your hands. Hold this position for 20 to 30 seconds. This is a good stretch for the forearms.

Wrist Roll-Up Behind Back

In this variation of the wrist curl, you'll be standing and using either a barbell or dumbbell. Use a thinner barbell rather than a regular-width Olympic or powerlifter barbell. You want the barbell to roll off your

fingers, and the thinner bars give you more movement (more distance to roll the weight up and down).

Position the barbell behind your back and keep your arms locked and straight. Only the hands must move during the exercise. Don't cheat by bending your elbows. With the barbell in your hands, slowly open your hands and let the barbell roll down until it reaches the ends of your fingers. Then slowly roll the barbell back up into your palms and close your hands as you bring them as far as you can toward your forearms. Again, only the hands must move. Hold the barbell in this fully contracted position for 2 to 3 seconds, then slowly lower it again and repeat.

After you've done your last rep and last set, place the palms of your hands against a wall and raise your

Wrist roll-up behind back (a)

Wrist roll-up behind back (b)

arms higher than your hands. Hold the position for 20 to 30 seconds. This is a good stretch for the forearms.

Use light weights and go for high reps. In fact, don't even count reps.

Keep doing a set until you can no longer move the weight up at all. To use dumbbells instead of a barbell, simply hold a dumbbell in each hand and follow the instructions.

23

The *Bodybuilding 201* Quads Exercises

For the leg exercises I am going to split things up by giving you quad exercises first, followed by hamstrings and calves in the next two chapters.

Leg Press

Pick a weight that you'll be able to do for 8 to 10 reps. Place your feet on the platform with a wide stance and your toes angled slightly outward. Stay tight in the seat and don't let your glutes come up and off the seat during the movement. Lower the weight down until your knees are near shoulder level and away from your body. Always keep your knees in a direct line over your big toes when lowering or pushing the weight. Rest no longer than 45 seconds between sets.

Front Squat with Heels Elevated

Warm up by doing a set of 20 to 25 brisk knee bends. After the warm-up, place a barbell across your collarbone. Position your heels on either a 1-inch wood block or two 25-pound plates (one heel on each plate). Allow your knees to bend and your upper body to come down until your upper legs are

Leg press (a)

Leg press (b)

Front squat with heels elevated (a)

Front squat with heels elevated (b)

about parallel with the floor (just as if you were doing a regular squat). Keep your upper body erect, head up and looking forward. Remember, just like a machine: up, down, up, down, no rest between reps.

Single-Quad Leg Press

For this exercise, you simply do a regular leg press with one leg at a time. It's pretty much the same movement, but you'll use much lighter weight (50 percent less than you'd use for both legs) and you'll use two foot positions:

Single-quad leg press (a)

- Foot turned slightly outward and placed near the outer edge of the platform
- Foot placed in the center of the platform and pointed straight up and down

This exercise also works more than one muscle group—in this case, quads and calves. You can use either a vertical, 45-degree, or 30-degree leg press.

Single-quad leg press (b)

Bend your knees and lower the platform until your glutes are *almost* ready to come up and out of the seated start position. Your upper thighs should be roughly straight up and down and almost in the vertical 90-degree position.

Use a slower and very controlled movement when exercising one leg at a time. Heavy weights and speed aren't as important here as isolation and focusing on making one leg at a time work intensely by doing nonstop and nonlockout reps.

Leg Extension

While this exercise is not known for being a mass builder, it is a good strength builder, especially around the connective tissue of the knee. Your strength can be severely limited by your weakest link in the exercise chain, so keeping the area around your knees strong and flexible is very important.

Keep the backs of your legs (around the knee area) firmly against the seat. Fully extend your legs in front

Leg extension (a)

Leg extension (b)

of you and squeeze really hard as you contract the muscle. Hold your legs in this contracted position for 1 to 2 seconds, then slowly lower the legs down and repeat. Rest no longer than 30 seconds between sets. For a more intense movement try bringing your upper body forward and leaning over your quads while you execute the movement.

Smith Machine Squat with Feet Wide and Pointed Out

Your legs are already good and warmed up, so load the bar with just enough weight for you to be able to do a set of 25 reps. Your feet should be a little wider than shoulder-width apart and your feet should be pointed outward and away from the body.

Rest the bar on the top of your traps and across the tops of your delts. Keep your upper body erect, neck and head up and looking forward. Bend your knees and allow the bar to come down, keeping the knees in a straight line over the toes. Stop your descent just above the parallel position. Feel it really stretch your inner thighs and glutes. Because the feet are so wide you won't need to go down to parallel to get great results.

Machine Hack Squat

The machine hack squat is really a great movement, especially if it's preceded by a warm-up with the stationary bike.

Load enough weights on the machine so that you can do 15 to 19 reps with strict good form, but when you hit the fifteenth rep your legs will be burning like crazy.

Vary the foot position, too. Place your feet high up toward the top of the foot platform and keep them in that general location, even when changing foot position.

Smith machine squat with feet wide and pointed out (a)

Smith machine squat with feet wide and pointed out (b)

Machine hack squat with feet shoulder-width apart

Machine hack squat with feet shoulder-width apart

Machine hack squat with feet wide and pointed out

Machine hack squat with feet narrow

If you do 15 reps, do 5 reps with feet wide apart and knees always traveling over the big toes; 5 reps with feet about 8 to 10 inches apart and straight forward, but with heels up and off the foot platform and all the weight centered over the balls and front of your feet; and 5 reps with knees and feet together and heels and toes on the platform.

Keep the legs moving; don't stop between reps or do the reps too slowly. Picture your legs like pistons in an engine that are constantly moving up and down.

Sissy Squat

This is one of those exercises that looks easy when you watch someone else do it, but when you try it you quickly find out there's nothing sissy about it except the name.

To get used to the feel of the exercise, you might want to do sissy squats with a bench (as illustrated in the photos). From there it's time to graduate to the real McCoy. The key to making this exercise work is to keep the legs together, the knees traveling in a straight line over the feet, and the upper body in a straight line with the legs, and to do nonstop, non-lockout reps.

Use only your bodyweight. Put your legs and feet together. Keep your upper body in a straight line with your legs. With either one or both hands, hold onto a wall or machine or both sides of the rack inside a squat rack. Bend the knees and bring your legs forward so that your knees come over the feet. Your legs and upper body need to be at a 40- to 60-degree angle when doing this movement. Get as close as you can to that angle and keep your body in that position from start to finish.

You may find it easy to remember what angle your body should be in by looking at the angle of the racks (where the foot plate slides up and down) on a leg press or hack squat machine. Shoot for keeping your body in that angle range because this will make the sissy squat much more intense and effective for you.

Make your legs do the work as they lower and raise your body over your feet. Try to use your hands only for balance. Lower your body as far down as you comfortably can and raise it up only to the three-quarters-lockout position. Don't go for a full lockout, because this will take the work off the legs. High reps (more than 15) are recommended.

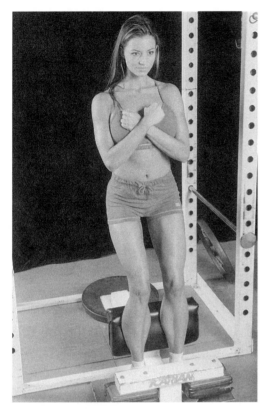

Sissy squat with bench (a)

Sissy squat with bench (b)

Sissy squat (a)

Sissy squat (b)

RESEARCH UPDATE: Squats and Your Back

New research shows that squats—often criticized as being "bad for your back"—could actually do your spine some good. In many modern health clubs, the popularity of exercise machines has left the squat rack relegated to a dark, dusty corner in the back of the gym. However, this recent trial shows that squats (and other related exercises, such as the deadlift) could be the best way to maintain the strength of your spine as you get older.

The study, published in the *International Journal of Sports Medicine*,* examined the back of the man who held the world record for the squat. Several scans revealed a remarkably healthy spine in this man who could squat over 1,000 pounds. MRI scans revealed normal spinal alignment. There was no evidence of disk herniation or compressive disk disease. More important,

the scans also showed an extremely high level of bone strength (called bone mineral density) in the spine.

This is important, especially for women. According to some estimates, 1 out of every 3 women over the age of 65 will suffer a fracture of the spine. A reduced bone mineral density—which increases the risk of a fracture—is far more widespread than previously thought. Recent surveys show that almost 4 out of 10 women aged 50 or over have osteopenia, which is a mild bone mineral loss.

When calcium in your diet runs short, the body drains the calcium stored in your bones. This weakens them significantly. Some bones, especially those in the spine, can become so weak that just the weight of your body causes them to suddenly disintegrate, often into scattered fragments that can't be reassembled. Your spine can also become "compressed" during old age, forming what is often called a dowager's

hump. This is the posture assumed by many older women as they appear to get shorter.

When squatting with a heavy weight, be sure to avoid the popular recommendation to keep your back flat. According to Dr. Mel Siff, in his book *Facts and Fallacies of Fitness*, a flat back is "virtually impossible" for most normal people to achieve: "Keeping the back 'flat' is common advice in the gymnasium training environment, yet its validity is rarely questioned. Actually, a flat back devoid of any curvature, is not only virtually impossible for a normal person to achieve, but it also reduces the ability of the spine to absorb or distribute shock and stress effectively." Although there are numerous factors affecting the strength of your bones, training with heavy weights is one of the best ways to ensure you're still leading an active life right into old age.

* Dickerman, R. D., R. Pertusi, and G. H. Smith. "The Upper Range of Lumbar Spine Bone Mineral Density: An Examination of the Current World Record Holder in the Squat Lift." *International Journal of Sports Medicine* 21 (2002): 469–70.

24

The *Bodybuilding 201* Hamstrings Exercises

A rule of thumb for leg exercises is to always do an equal amount of work (i.e., sets, reps, weight) for front and back. With these exercises you'll have the back of the legs well covered, with plenty to spare.

Kneeling Body Sway

Get ready for a big surprise: the toughest hamstring exercise you'll *ever* do uses no machine and no weight. This is a killer.

Start by kneeling on the floor with your knees and legs together. Have a partner hold your ankles. While keeping your legs and upper body erect (imagine a big steel pin running through you from your head to your knees), slowly let your body lean forward a few inches and then bring it back to the vertical starting position. Go only a few inches at first until you feel strong enough and comfortable enough to allow the body to go farther forward. I suggest holding on to a barbell or vertical support until your hamstrings are strengthened sufficiently to do this exercise without it.

Kneeling body sway (a)

You will be shocked at how difficult it is to go only a few inches forward. I suggest positioning your body about 1 to 2 feet away from a wall so that you can touch the wall with your hands and use it to push off if you get

Kneeling body sway (b)

Kneeling body sway with vertical support (a)

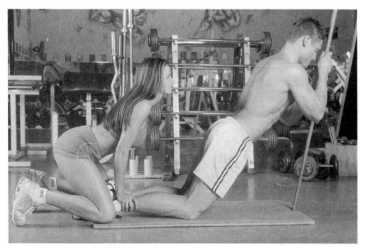

Kneeling body sway with vertical support (b)

stuck or have difficulty bringing your body back up to the starting position.

This is a phenomenal back leg exercise because it uses your body-weight and gravity as resistance; the only muscles resisting your body's movement forward and pulling it back up are your hamstrings. You must keep your upper body erect from start to finish and not cheat by bending forward or backward at the waist.

Be sure to stretch your hamstrings *before* doing this exercise! And get ready for them to cramp. Even if you're doing heavy stiff-legged dead-lifts, hamstring curls, or any other hamstring exercises, your hamstrings will *not* be used to this kind of direct intensity, so take it slow.

Do this exercise no more than one workout every three weeks! Do all the other hamstring exercises between then, but limit this one. No exceptions. It's that intense.

Leg Curl

With this exercise, it's good to go for the reps. Be sure to keep your stomach tight and against the pad as you execute the movement. Always do full-range-of-motion reps—stretch fully when you extend your legs and con-tract as you curl the weight up toward your glutes. Keep the reps going non-stop until you've finished all your reps for the set.

Hyper Bench Leg Curl

This exercise will work not just the hamstrings but the lower back and glutes. Lie on your stomach on the hyper bench, positioning your upper body off the bench and forward enough that you're able to use a full range of motion. Bend forward at the waist, allowing only the upper body to move. Lower the upper torso until you get a good stretch, and then raise it until it is parallel to the floor and in a

Leg curl (a)

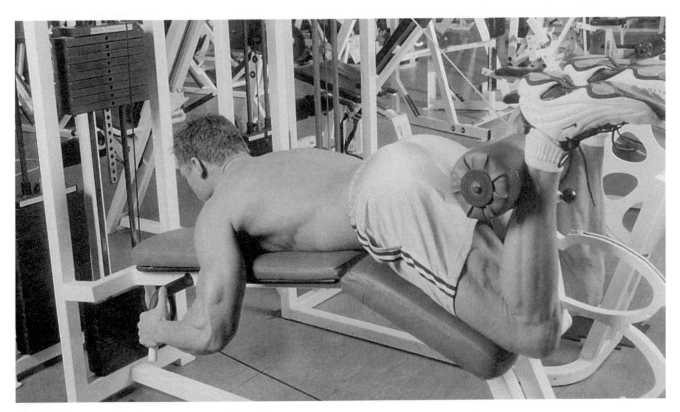

Leg curl (b)

Hyper bench leg curl (a)

Hyper bench leg curl (b)

straight line with your legs. Really contract the lower back, hamstrings, and glutes at the top of the movement.

Barbell Stiff-Legged Deadlift

The leg curl is not a bad exercise if it's the only one you can do. But if you want a terrific hamstrings movement, you need to try the stiff-legged deadlift. It works not only the hamstrings but the traps, shoulders, forearms, and lower back. To get the best results, perfect form (or as close to it as you can get) is a must. This will not only prevent injury but isolate the hamstrings and hit those deep muscle fibers.

Stand on a wooden platform elevated at least 4 inches, or on a flat bench. Take a shoulder-width grip on a barbell. You may use an overhand grip or a combination grip (one hand over and one hand under).

Holding the weight with your arms locked and your body fully erect, bend the upper torso over until the bar is lowered as far as possible. With arms locked throughout the movement, bring your upper torso back up to the fully upright and erect position. Rest no longer than 45 seconds between sets, and do not rest between reps.

The following tips will help you get the most out of this exercise.

- Go as far as you can to get a good stretch. Some people will be able to lower the bar until it touches the top of their feet; others may be able to bring the barbell only to shin level.
- You may bend your knees, but only slightly.
- Make sure the hamstrings are fully stretched.
- Do not round your back as you lower the weight. Keep your back tight; this is not a lat movement.
- Use a controlled movement throughout the entire rep; never bounce or jerk your body or the weight.
- Keep the barbell close to your body from start to finish.

Barbell stiff-legged deadlift (a)

Barbell stiff-legged deadlift (b)

Dumbbell Stiff-Legged Deadlift

If you don't have a barbell or just want some variety, try dumbbell stiff-legged deadlifts. The big difference with this variation is your arm and hand position when you bend over. This exercise will work the lower back, traps, forearms, hamstrings, and glutes. As with the barbell version of this exercise, I recommend standing on a platform to give you more room to stretch.

Select a pair of dumbbells that are about 30 percent of your bodyweight (for example, a 150-pound person would use 45-pound dumbbells). To get the best results, perfect form (or as close to it as you can get) is a must. This will not only prevent injury but also isolate the hamstrings and hit those deep muscle fibers.

Holding the weight with your arms locked out to your sides and your body fully erect, bend the upper torso over until the weights are lowered as far down as possible.

The position of your arms and hands when you bend over is important: bring your arms around in front of you until the dumbbells and your palms are facing your shins.

For a great hamstrings stretch, lower the dumbbells on the last rep of your set and keep them in the lowered position for 20 to 30 seconds. Keep both legs together and feet pointed straight forward.

How far down should you go? Simply bring your upper body down as far as possible until you really feel a great stretch in your hamstrings. Don't bounce. Go as far as you comfortably can and you'll find your range of motion improving as you include this stretch in your routine on a regular basis.

Dumbbell stiff-legged deadlift (a)

Dumbbell stiff-legged deadlift (b)

25

The *Bodybuilding 201* Calves Exercises

While there is little you can do to change the genetic shape of your calves, there is a lot you can do to change how they look. Here are some great ways to do it.

Assisted Donkey Calf Raise

Very few bodybuilders have great calves. This is mostly due to genetics, but partly because they work calves at the very end of the workout and they don't do the best exercises for calves. So try working them at the beginning of your workout and using donkey calf raises.

The variation I suggest requires having a partner sit on your lower back while you execute the movement. The stretch and burn you will feel will be incredible.

Place your toes and the balls of your feet on a 4-inch block of wood. Be sure the block is high enough so that you can lower your heels all the way down for a full stretch without touching the floor.

While keeping your legs straight and knees locked, bend your upper

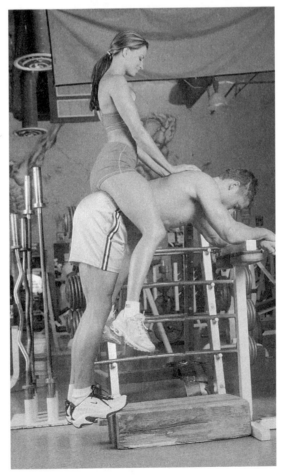

Assisted donkey calf raise (a)

Assisted donkey calf raise (b)

body forward until it is at a 90-degree angle. To support your upper body, rest your forearms and elbows on a flat bench or rack of dumbbells.

Have your training partner sit on top of your lower back, centered almost at the very end of your lower back so that his or her body is in line right above your glutes and legs. The farther back your partner sits, the more you will feel it in your calves. Slowly lower your heels for a good stretch and hold for 1 to 2 seconds. Then slowly raise your heels up until you are on the tips of your toes and hold for 1 to 2 seconds. Repeat the lowering-raising movement until you've done 10 reps. Rest for no longer than 30 to 45 seconds.

After you've done the sets and reps, with your partner still on your back, lower your heels again, keep your legs and knees locked, and stretch your calves in that position for 30 to 60 seconds.

Standing Calf Raise

Place the balls of your feet on the ends of the platform of the calf raise machine. Keep your body erect and move only your feet and ankles throughout the exercise. Pick a weight that is at least 50 percent heavier than your bodyweight. Allow the weight to lower your heels all the way down to the floor below the platform in order to get a great stretch. Hold the weight in this position for 1 to 2 seconds, then raise up on your toes until your calves are fully contracted at the top position. The important thing to remember is the stretch at the bottom and the contraction at the top of the movement. Do 10 to 12 reps per set. Rest no longer than 30 seconds between sets.

Leg Press Toe Raise

Assume a position as if you were doing a regular leg press. Instead of placing your feet high up on the platform, place only the balls of the feet on the very lower edge or the bottom of the platform. *Keep your knees completely locked. This is very important.* Let the weight come down a few inches until your toes come back as far as possible. This is the bottom, or the fully stretched, position. Hold the weight there for 1 to 2 seconds, then push it up with your feet until the calves are fully contracted and the weight will not go any farther. Rest only 30 seconds between sets.

After you've done your last set, stretch your calves. Find a platform that will allow you to lower your heels as far as possible without touching the

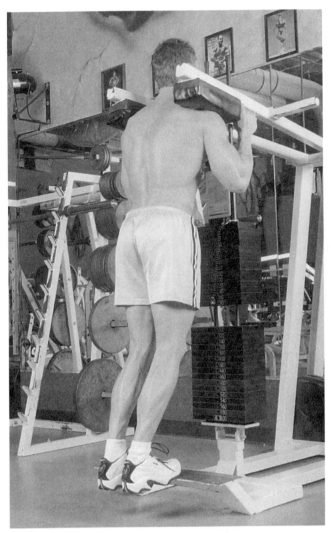

Standing calf raise (a)

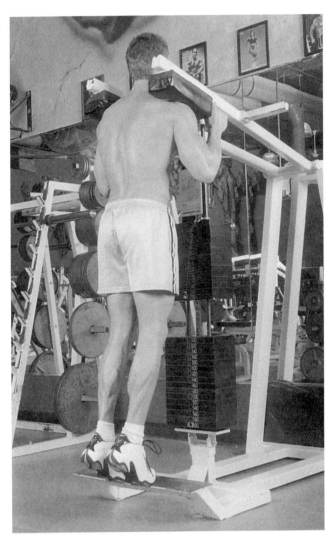

Standing calf raise (b)

Leg press toe raise (a)

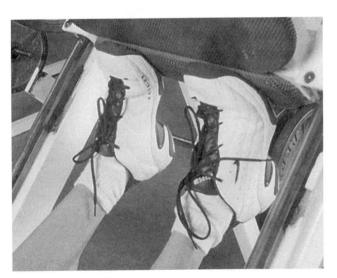

Leg press toe raise (b)

floor. Stay in this fully stretched position for at least 50 seconds. Do this after every calf workout and watch what happens to your calves!

Seated Calf Raise

Pick a weight on the seated calf raise machine that will allow you to do 25 to 45 reps. Place the balls of your feet on the end of the foot platform and the upper leg pad just above the upper knee. Lower your heels until they reach maximal stretch, then raise them until they are maximally contracted. Slowly lower and repeat for 1 set of 25 to 45 reps. Always stretch the calves after the last set.

Standing Toe Raise

This is such a great calf exercise and it doesn't require a machine or any weight—just your bodyweight and a platform of any kind. A few things to remember:

- You need to get a great stretch at the bottom and a big contraction at the top of the exercise. Work the calf in its complete range of motion.
- Put only the front of the balls of your feet on the platform so that you'll be able to get the full range of motion.
- Keep your feet about 10 to 12 inches apart and your knees touching each other throughout the exercise.
- Really concentrate on shifting your bodyweight so that you feel it over the big toes. This will focus the calf work so that it hits the inner calf and will help you get that nice diamond shape.

All that's left is doing the reps, so continue the movement until your calves really start burning. Don't stop until you've hit 40 to 60 reps. Go for more if you can. You'll find that as you do these bodyweight-only calf raises, not only will your calf shape change,

Seated calf raise (a)

Seated calf raise (b)

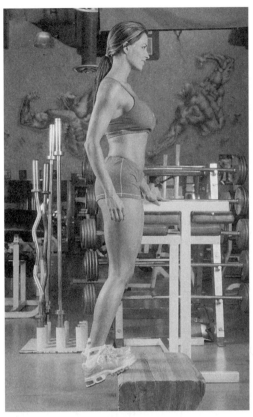

Standing toe raise (side view) (a)

Standing toe raise (side view) (b)

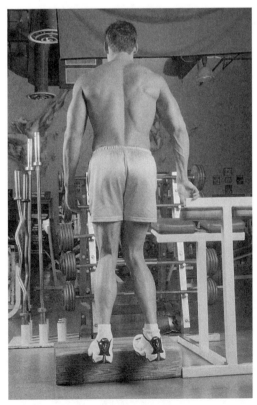

Standing toe raise (rear view) (c)

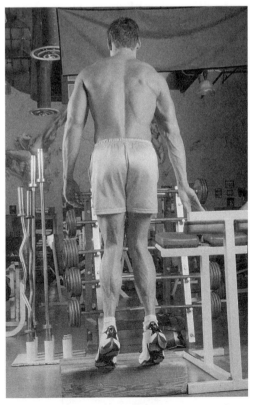

Standing toe raise (rear view) (d)

so will your ability to do more and more reps.

Instead of waiting to stretch at the end of the workout, do your calf stretch immediately after your last rep. Stand on the edge of the same platform you used for the calf raise. Keep your body straight and hold on to something for balance only if you need to, but not to take your bodyweight off the stretched calf muscles. This will really burn, and that's exactly what you want. Hold the stretched position for 20 to 30 seconds.

Stairclimber Calf Raise

You are going to be surprised at just how well this cardio exercise will build and define your calves. Follow all my tips in Chapter 31 on using the stairclimber, with this exception. First, try not to hold on to the side handrails. Doing so takes resistance off your body. Instead, do these keeping your hands free and moving back and forth,

just like you would if you were walking or running up the stairs.

Next, bring your toes as far back as possible so that they are on the edge of the step platform and your heels are completely off the foot platform, never touching it.

As you begin the stepping movement up and down, go all the way up and all the way down. When the leg comes up, stand up as high as you can on your toes and fully contract the calf with that foot. When the leg and platform come down, straighten your leg and lower the heel down as far as possible for the deep calf stretch. Do this on every step.

Vary your pace and position: do a few minutes of full up-and-down stepping, taking longer between steps and half-steps, then do much faster partial steps of only a few inches up and down, moving very quickly between steps. Thirty days from now, you'll be thanking me.

Stairclimber calf raise (a)

Stairclimber calf raise (b)

26

The *Bodybuilding 201* Abs Exercises

Do one or two of the following ab
exercises each workout, but don't use
the same ab exercises in consecutive
workouts. Don't rest between reps and
don't allow the abs to relax. The only
rest the abs get are the 15 to 20
seconds between sets and the time you
take between exercises. Think constant
tension and short range of movement
and your abs will respond beautifully!

Crunch

More than likely you have done a
crunch at some point in your training.
However, many people do them incorrectly. Proper execution includes using
only a slight range of movement and
doing lots of reps with minimal rest
between sets.

As you do the crunch, bring your
upper body forward and crunch the
abs as far as possible, then allow the
body to come back down only about
3 to 4 inches before you come up and
crunch the abs again.

Many people come forward and
then allow their upper bodies to come

Crunch (a)

Crunch (b)

all the way down to the floor before they start again. This is not very effective. The abs work best when you keep constant tension in them, and well-executed crunches will really make them work! I've found that higher reps—more than 30 per set—work great. Rest no longer than 30 seconds between sets.

Rocking Crunch

Lie on the floor or on a flat bench with your legs up, knees bent, and legs together. Raise your upper body and bring it forward toward your knees while bringing your legs up and back toward your chin. At the top position, your body should be approaching the shape of a U or V.

On the next rep, don't bring your legs so far back, but bring your upper body farther forward as if trying to touch your knees with your upper body. On the third rep, don't bring your upper body so far up and forward; instead, bring your legs and knees back farther, as though trying to touch your chin. The rep cadence goes as follows:

- First rep: Equal distance up for lower and upper body
- Second rep: Upper body farther forward and legs lowered but not touching the floor or bench
- Third rep: Upper body lowered and not touching the floor or bench; legs and knees back to try to touch the chin

Do 4 sets of 30 reps (10 reps each way per set).

Bicycle Crunch

This is quite similar to the regular crunch. As you come forward to crunch your upper torso, allow the knees to come back toward your chest at the same time and do small, circular, pedaling-type motions. For variation, you can do a normal forward crunch,

Rocking crunch (a)

Rocking crunch (b)

Bicycle crunch (a)

Bicycle crunch (b)

an alternating one side up/the other side up crunch, or a combination of left side/forward/right side bicycle crunch. Do 4 sets of 30 to 50 reps. Rest no longer than 15 to 20 seconds between sets.

As with all ab work, especially crunches, use short-range movements of only a few inches from start to finish and keep the reps going without resting. This will make the abs burn and work very effectively.

Assisted Seated Crunch

Most people think crunches are a good exercise for shaping up the midsection, and that's true. This crunch variation, in which a partner holds your calves against a flat bench, will let you really feel those abs working.

Lie on the floor on your back with your knees bent and your calves resting on top of a flat bench. Have a training partner either hold your ankles down against the bench or sit on top of your calves and ankles while you do the exercise. Place your arms either folded across your chest or clasped together behind your head.

Roll your upper torso forward as high as you can and crunch. At the top position, hold for 1 to 2 seconds, then very slowly allow your upper torso to come back down and straighten out. Allow it to unroll and come back down only slightly; you must keep constant tension in the abs. Keep your upper torso elevated and off the floor at the bottom position and hold it for 1 to 2 seconds before crunching and coming back up again.

The trick to really feeling this is to do very slow reps and keep your upper body up and off the floor at all times. Rest only 25 to 35 seconds between sets.

Reverse Hyperextension

This exercise is similar to the hyperextension exercise, but you lie on your

Assisted seated crunch (a)

Assisted seated crunch (b)

Reverse hyperextension (a)

Reverse hyperextension (b)

back rather than on your stomach and you don't bend as far. The movement is also similar to a crunch.

Lie on your back on the hyperextension bench with only the lower body on the bench. Allow the upper torso to come down only until it is parallel with the floor. Bend the head and chest upward and slightly forward. Continue to bring the upper body up and forward in this tucked position until you feel a maximum contraction in the abs. This should take only a few inches of movement if you're doing it correctly. Hold this contracted position for 2 to 3 seconds, then slowly, and I mean slowly, lower it back down a few inches and then right back up again. You should really feel the abs burn once you hit the 15-rep mark. Go for 1 set of at least 20 to 40 reps.

Trunk Twist

Many people who do ab exercises with resistance find their waistlines expanding instead of getting smaller. This is simply because they're stimulating the muscles in the ab/waist area, which causes them to get bigger and thicker instead of getting firmer, toned, tighter, and smaller. To avoid this, do trunk twists without weight or with a broomstick. You may do these either seated or standing.

Start with slow, limited-range-of-motion twists and increase the tempo and range of motion after 1 to 2 minutes of twisting. Do 3 to 5 minutes of continuous trunk twists.

Seated Trunk Twist with Legs Forward and Feet Elevated

This might feel weird at first, but don't worry—you'll get used to it. You'll use three increasingly difficult positions. First, sit on a flat bench with your legs and feet completely extended in front of you so that only your heels touch the floor. Next, increase the difficulty by keeping your knees slightly bent and feet off the ground. Finally, bend your knees more and bring your knees and legs up higher and toward your upper body.

Trunk twist (a)

Trunk twist (b)

You might be able to do only a couple of reps like this at first, but it'll get easier each time you do it. In no time you will be able to do side-to-side seated trunk twists with your knees up high and tucked close to your body. Talk about having great balance!

Seated trunk twist with legs forward and heels on the ground

Seated trunk twist with legs forward and feet elevated

Seated trunk twist with knees bent and up (a)

Seated trunk twist with knees bent and up (b)

Standing Trunk Twist with a Broomstick

Stand with your feet firmly on the floor, about shoulder-width apart. Place a broomstick behind your neck and grip each end with one hand, then begin twisting from side to side.

Lying Knee-Up

Do these on a flat bench or platform that's at least 12 inches off the floor. Lie on your back with only your glutes and upper body on the bench. Place your hands, palms down, under your glutes. Keep both legs together and allow your legs to straighten out in front of you so that they form a straight line with the upper body. Bend the knees and bring the legs up until they come to about stomach level. Contract the abs and slowly return the legs to the straightened position. Repeat. Keep the legs completely off the floor from start to finish. Do 4 sets of 20 to 30 reps.

Standing trunk twist with broomstick (a)

Standing trunk twist with broomstick (b)

Standing trunk twist with broomstick (c)

Lying knee-up (a)

Hanging Knee-Up

This is a great exercise for the lower abs. Hang from a chin-up bar that's high enough off the ground that you can hang straight up and down without your feet touching the floor. With hands about shoulder-width apart, take an overhand grip on a chinning bar. Keeping your upper torso erect, raise your upper legs so that your knees come up and toward your stomach area. Try raising them straight up in front of you, then up to your right and left. Really make the abdominals contract as your legs come up and your lower torso bends slightly forward and upward. Think of your body as forming a U-shape. Lower and repeat. Do 1 set of as many reps as possible. Don't get discouraged if you can't do many right now. You will soon enough.

Lying knee-up (b)

Hanging knee-up (a)

Hanging knee-up (b)

Hanging knee-up (c)

Hanging knee-up (d)

RESEARCH UPDATE:
Abdominal Workout Myths

In an attempt to flatten the stomach, most people spend their abdominal workouts trying to "isolate" their abdominal muscles. Of course, the most effective abdominal workout in the world will do you no good if your abdominals are hidden under a layer of fat. The first step to a flatter stomach is a good diet, combined with an effective exercise program specifically designed for fat loss.

Abdominal Workouts

Over the past few years numerous routines and techniques have been promoted as ways to make your abdominal workouts more effective. Bending your knees during the sit-up, for example, is recommended as a way to reduce the activity of the muscles that flex your hip, which in turn is supposed to reduce the stress to your lower back and lead to greater isolation of the abdominals. It's a myth that's very popular today, despite research showing that moving the legs from straight to bent actually increases hip flexor activity.

Pressing your heels into the floor during the sit-up is also said to "disable" the psoas, one of the muscles responsible for flexing your hips. A reduction in psoas activity is thought to "isolate" your abdominals and reduce the risk of injury to the spine. Press-heel sit-ups are performed in the same way as a regular sit-up. The only difference is that as you raise your upper body, you press your heels into the floor.

Press-Heel Sit-Ups

The press-heel sit-up does have a reputation as the best way to "isolate" your abdominals. Yet there's very little evidence to show that it reduces psoas activity. In fact, a research team from the University of Bern in Switzerland has found that the exact opposite occurs! The study, reported in the journal *Medicine and Science in Sports and Exercise*,* compared a number of different abdominal exercises using electrodes inserted into vertebral portions of the psoas and three layers of the abdominal wall. The results showed that muscle activity in the psoas was slightly higher during the press-heel sit-up compared to the bent-knee sit-up.

It's important to note that this research didn't test other variations of the press-heel sit-up. For instance, rather than press your heels into the floor, your training partner can place his or her hands under your calves. As you sit up, you then pull against the partner's hands with your legs.

However, even if this could "disable" the psoas muscle, certain movements are *meant* to involve both the hip and trunk flexors. There's very little evidence to show that anyone with a healthy spine needs to avoid exercises that work both muscle groups simultaneously. The fact that it's so difficult to perform a sit-up *without* working both the hip and trunk flexors shows that these muscles were designed to work together.

Twisting

One of the other "secrets" revealed in the study was that the muscles on both sides of your waist (called the obliques) are highly active during both the press-heel sit-up and the regular sit-up. To "tone" these muscles, most people add a small twist to the end of a sit-up, which actually serves very little purpose. If you want to work the obliques a little harder during the sit-up, twisting movements are most effective when the twist is initiated at the *start*, rather than at the *end*, of a sit-up.

---

* Juker, D., S. McGill, P. Kropf, and T. Steffen. "Quantitative Intramuscular Myoelectric Activity of Lumbar Portions of Psoas and the Abdominal Wall During a Wide Variety of Tasks." *Medicine and Science in Sports and Exercise* 30 (1998): 301–10.

PART VI

Bodybuilding 201
Specialization Exercises

27

My Favorite Workouts for the *Bodybuilding 201* Athlete

Of all the information I'm giving you about how to think right and train right, workouts for each bodypart are perhaps one of the most important things I can share—workouts I used to put on more than 60 pounds of muscle in two years. Yes, you've heard me repeat this a few times in this book, but I want you to know that you really can make great gains if you train right, eat right, and do it naturally. I know these workouts work incredibly well, not only from my own experience but from that of all the people who've used them in training with me over the years.

One of the best training partners I've ever had was a guy named Tom Walden. Tom is 10 years older than I am, and he grew up on the streets and had that "street toughness" about him. To hang with "Waldy," especially to train with him, you needed to be prepared for battle, because if you didn't push him he would be in your face pushing you. And because of that, he was the perfect training partner for me. Each workout, he'd come in the gym and not know what we were

about to do or what I was about to throw at him. And we both loved that element of surprise and our daily test to see who would be the stronger one that day.

We trained *very* hard, and others in the gym would often stop and watch and ask us questions. And they loved the camaraderie, even after all the abuse (in a fun way) we'd throw at them for being wusses and not training hard enough to get results. Each day, they came into that gym and waited not only to hear Tom and me ribbing each other but to find out whether they were going to be our next victim. And you know what? Anyone who trained in our gym at that time can remember those days and say those were good times.

In many of the gyms across the country I've trained in, it's a much different scene. The clubs look great but people rarely talk to each other. They're in their own little private world, doing their own little private arm curl, and few are getting truly noticeable results. They pay their dues, they go to the gym each week, and

161

they pretty much look and feel the same, week after week, year after year.

It's time to change that. It's time to break out of your cocoon, mix it up, get a little edge to your training, and charge up the atmosphere around you.

Looking back over my training logs and notes, I see that I often asked those who were much stronger than I to train with me or spot me. The adrenaline and positive pressure and reinforcement from being around such great lifters rocketed my poundages and gains until I was in their league and even surpassed them.

The same strategy can work wonders for you, too. It's an amazing thing if you're a 300-pound squatter who trains with 500-, 600-, and 700-pound squatters to watch how quickly your size and strength go up just by training with and being inspired by them.

MY BEST WORKOUTS

I looked back over my training log and found the workouts that kicked my butt and produced major results. I noticed some very interesting things about those workouts:

- Most of the best workouts I had were based on a four-day split in which I trained on Monday, Tuesday, Thursday, and Friday (rest days were Wednesday, Saturday, and Sunday).
- The workouts were divided into push and pull. On Monday and Thursday, I would train chest, shoulders, and triceps. On Tuesday and Friday, I'd train legs, back, and biceps.
- Rarely would I do any direct ab work because all the various exercises and weight I used indirectly worked the abs very effectively. Try keeping your upper body erect with your elbows into your sides while doing a straight-bar triceps pressdown with

200 pounds for reps and you'll see what I mean about working the abs *without* working the abs.

- The workouts were divided into heavy-day training and moderate-day training. Mondays and Tuesdays were heavy days, and Thursdays and Fridays were moderate-weight days.
- Each year I trained approximately 40 to 45 weeks and took 3 to 7 days off from training every 4 to 6 weeks.
- I trained five bodyparts (chest, back, shoulders, arms, legs) two times per week for 40 to 45 weeks per year, and in that year I would do more than 400 different workouts. Sometimes these workout differences were huge and sometimes they were only slight, but rarely would I do the same workout twice.
- Every time in the gym, I would do something a little different. This kept me motivated, excited to train, and really looking forward to my next workout. It also kept my body growing and getting stronger.
- I found that my body responded so well to supersets that I included them in nearly every workout.

You're about to see a sample of exactly what I did (along with amount of weights used on many of those workouts) during one of my most productive one-year periods of training.

I'm going to give you 51 bodypart workouts that I know will give you terrific results. Yet this is only a fraction of the thousands of workouts I have recorded in my training log. I strongly encourage you to start keeping your own log that you'll be able to refer back to. If you ever get into a rut in your training, you might find it helpful to look back at your log and try some of the workout techniques and tactics that proved effective for you in the past.

28

51 Workouts That'll Pack On Serious Size and Strength

Make sure you read the chapters on warming up, stretching, and cooling down before using any of the following workouts. Besides all the other things I did before each workout, I'd always stretch, do a mimic of the exercise with no weights to warm up, and do a light- to moderate-weight warm-up set before jumping up to my heavier sets.

Workout 1 (Chest)

Heavy dumbbell inclines: 5 sets of 5 with 105

Machine inclines: 5 sets of 10 slow reps with 145

Dumbbell incline flyes: 3 sets of 8 with 70

Cable crunches: 3 sets of 8 with 70

Workout 2 (Triceps)

Bent-over rope extensions: 5 sets of 10

Superset lying EZ-bar French presses (5 sets of 10 with 80) to seated straight-bar French presses (5 sets of 10 with 50)

Workout 3 (Legs)

Leg presses: 5 sets of 12 with 560

Leg curls: 7 sets of 10 with 90 down to 40

Squats: 5 sets of 10 with 325

Sissy squats: 6 sets of 20

Standing calf raises: 4 sets of 8 up to 500

Workout 4 (Biceps)

Wide-grip barbell curls: 5 sets of 10 up to 110

EZ-curl preacher curls: 5 sets of 10–15 with 70

Workout 5 (Back)

Superset chins with close-grip front pulldowns: 4 sets of 8–10

Close-grip T-bar rows: 4 sets of 9 with six 35-pound plates

Workout 6 (Chest)

Incline bench presses: 6 sets of 8–10, up to 245 for 3 reps

Dumbbell incline flyes: 5 sets of 8 with 70

Dips: 3 sets of 10

Workout 7 (Triceps)

Superset lying EZ-bar French presses (5 sets of 8–10 with 80–90) to seated barbell French presses (5 sets of 8–10 with 70 down to 50)

Dumbbell triceps kickbacks: 4 sets of 12 with 30

Workout 8 (Legs)

Leg presses: 6 sets of 12 up to 560 for 3 reps

Leg curls: 5 sets of 8 up to 110 for 6 reps

Squats: 4 sets of 10 up to 300

Sissy squats: 6 sets of 20

Standing calf raises: 4 sets of 12–15 with entire stack

Seated calf raises: 5 sets of 15 up to seven 25-pound plates

Workout 9 (Biceps)
(Mr. Universe Dave Johns's routine)

Straight-bar curls on Scott bench: 6 sets of 10 to 70

Dumbbell Scott curls: 6 sets of 10, with 30, 30, 30, 25, 25, 25

Workout 10 (Back)

Superset wide-grip chin-ups (reps to limit) to close-grip pulldowns using T-style stirrup handle: 4 sets of 8 up to 190

T-bar rows: 4 sets of 8 with 6 35-pound plates

Seated rows: 4 sets of 12 with 180, 160, 160, 140

Workout 11 (Biceps)

Forced reps straight-bar curls on Scott bench: 8 sets of 10 with 60, 70, 80, 90, 80, 70, 60, 50

Workout 12 (Chest)

Incline barbell bench presses: 6 sets of 5 up to 225 for 2 sets

Machine bench presses: 5 sets of 5 with 300

Dumbbell incline flyes: 4 sets of 10 with 50, 20 seconds of rest between sets

Workout 13 (Calves)

Standing calf raises: 4 sets of 20 with partner-assisted pyramiding (200, 300, 400, 500)

Workout 14 (Triceps)

Superset lying EZ-bar French presses (8 reps with 80 pounds) to seated dumbbell French presses (8 reps with 70 pounds)

Close-grip straight-bar pushdowns: 4 sets of 12 with 50, 60, 70, 80

Workout 15 (Shoulders)

Seated dumbbell presses: 5 sets of 8 up to 55

Incline rear delt raises: 5 sets of reps to limit with 20

Seated dumbbell side laterals: 5 sets of 10 with 25

Barbell shrugs: 3 sets of 10 with 200

Workout 16 (Biceps)

Standing wide-grip barbell curls: 4 sets of 8 with 80, 90, 100, 100

Seated 45-degree dumbbell curls: 4 sets of 8 with 35, 35, 30, 30

One-arm dumbbell Scott curls: 4 sets of 12–20 with 35, 35, 30, 30

Workout 17 (Back)

Seated close-grip pulldowns (but into lower stomach, like doing seated cable rows): 6 sets of 12–15 up to 170

T-bar rows: 4 sets of 8 up to seven 35-pound plates

Bent-over barbell rows: 4 sets of 10 with 135

Workout 18 (Hamstrings)

Superset leg curls (10 reps with 130) to hyperextensions holding 45-pound plate (reps to limit): 5 supersets

Standing leg curls (5 sets of 8 with 70) to stiff-legged deadlifts (6 reps with 135)

Workout 19 (Biceps)

Performed superfast with quick reps and absolutely minimal rest between sets and exercises

Standing barbell curls: 4 sets of 8 up to 100

Seated (using fourth notch on bench) incline curls: 4 sets of 8 with 35, 35, 30, 30

Standing bent-over dumbbell concentration curls: 4 sets to limit with 35, 35, 30, 30

Workout 20 (Quads)

Machine squats: 6 sets of 12–15 with 275, after 2 warm-up sets

Hack squats: 4 sets to limit up to 200

Sissy squats: 4 sets of 20

Workout 21 (Chest)

Dumbbell inclines: 6 sets of 8 up to 110

Dumbbell incline flyes: 5 sets of 10 with 45, 50, 55, 50, 45

Workout 22 (Back)

Superset wide-grip pulldowns (160) to close-grip chins: 4 sets of 12 to limit

T-bar rows: 4 sets of 8 up to 6 35-pound plates for last set of 15 reps

Seated cable rows: 4 sets of 12 with 160

Workout 23 (Chest)

Dumbbell incline presses: 5 sets of 8 with 110

Dumbbell incline flyes: 5 sets of 8 with 55

Close-hand (one hand over the other hand) push-ups with feet on a bench: 4 sets of 15

Workout 24 (Back)

Superset close-grip pulldowns (to 170) to dumbbell pullovers (to 85): 4 supersets of 8–12

T-bar rows: 4 sets of 8 up to six 35-pound plates

Seated cable rows: 4 sets of 10–12 with 160

Workout 25 (Chest)

Dumbbell incline presses: 6 sets of 8–10 with 110, 100, 90, 80, 75, 75, after warm-up with 60

Machine dead-stop bench presses: 6 sets of 80 down to 10 with 275, 250, 225, 200, 200, 200

Flat bench dumbbell flyes: 4 sets of 8–10 with 50, 45, 40, 40

Workout 26 (Triceps)

Superset lying EZ-bar French presses (with 90) to seated dumbbell French presses (with 75): 5 supersets of 10–12 reps

Machine pressdowns with straight bar: 4 sets to limit with 80, 70, 60, 50

Workout 27 (Legs)

Superset leg curls (5 sets of 12 to 100) to hyperextensions (5 sets of 8 to 70)

Superset standing leg curls (4 sets of 12 to 60) to stiff-legged deadlifts (4 sets of 8 with 155): total of 9 back leg supersets

Hack squats: 4 sets of 15 with 200, 200, 175, 150

Machine standing calf raises: 8 sets of 12–15 up to 400, then back down to 200

Seated calf raises: 4 sets of 12–15 with 105

Workout 28 (Shoulders)

Superset machine presses (to 175) to standing dumbbell side laterals (35, 30, 25, 20, 20): 5 supersets of 10–12

Bent-over cable laterals: 5 sets of 12 with 40, 30, 30, 20, 20

Superset barbell shrugs (215) to upright rows (60): 4 supersets of 10–12

Workout 29 (Biceps)

Standing barbell curls: 5 sets of 8 with 80, 90, 100, 100, 100

Dumbbell Scott curls: 3 sets of 8–10 with 30

Seated concentration curls: 2 sets to limit with 35

Workout 30 (Back)

Superset wide-grip chin-ups (to limit) to medium-grip front pulldowns (140): 4 supersets of 10

T-bar rows: 3 sets of 8 with five 35-pound plates

Standing on bench cable straight-bar rows: 4 sets of 10–12 with 140, 160, 180, 200

Workout 31 (Shoulders)

Machine presses: 7 sets of 10 with 135 up to 190 down to 115

Seated one-arm side laterals: 5 sets of 12 with 25, 25, 20, 20, 20

Bent-over dumbbell laterals: 5 sets of 12 with 35

Upright EZ-bar rows: 5 sets of 10 with 110, 100, 90, 80, 70

Workout 32 (Triceps)

Seated dumbbell French presses with back against bench: 5 sets to limit with 70, 80, 80, 80, 70

Lying EZ-bar French presses: 4 sets to limit with 90

Rope triceps pressdowns: 4 sets to limit with 70, 60, 40, 30

Workout 33 (Muscle Shock Workout for Legs)

Machine squats: 15 sets of 10–12 reps with 135, 15 sets with 185, 6 sets with 225, 6 sets with 185

Standing calf machine raises: 4 sets of 15 with 200, 240, 200, 160

Lying leg curls: 5 sets of 10–12 with 60, 80, 60, 40, 20

Workout 34 (Back)

Superset wide-grip chins (to limit) to machine rows (150, 140, 130, 120, 120): 5 supersets of 10–12

Dumbbell rows: 5 sets of 10 with 80, 90, 100, 100, 100

Workout 35 (Biceps)

Barbell curls: 5 sets of 8 with 90, 90, 90, 80, 70

Scott bench EZ-bar curls: 3 sets of limit with 80

Standing EZ-bar curl trade-offs with partner: 10 reps with 70, 1 set each; 9 reps with 70, 1 set each, for a total of 9 trade-off sets

Workout 36 (Shoulders)

Seated flat bench dumbbell presses: 7 sets of 8 with 65

Tri-set front laterals (8 reps with 35) to side laterals (10 reps with 25) to bent-over laterals (10 reps with 35): 4 sets of tri-sets

Workout 37 (Biceps)

Standing heavy barbell curls: 3 sets of 6–8 with 145

Standing Scott bench EZ-bar curls: 4 sets of 8 with 90, 90, 80, 80

Standing dumbbell alternating curls: 4 sets of 10 with 40

Workout 38 (Triceps)

Dips: 5 sets of 15

Standing dumbbell French presses: 4 sets of 8–10 with 70, 80, 80, 70

Triceps pressdowns: 3 sets of 10 with 100, 90, 80

Workout 39 (Calves)

Superset machine standing calf raises (4 sets of 15 with 400) to bodyweight-only calf raises (4 sets of 20)

Workout 40 (Triceps)

Standing dumbbell French presses: 4 sets of 8 with 80, 90, 95, 85

Lying EZ-bar French presses: 4 sets of 10 with 100

Dumbbell kickbacks: 4 sets of 10 with 25

Workout 41 (Chest)

Flat bench presses: 6 sets of 6–10 up to 285

Dumbbell incline presses: 5 sets of 8 with 100, 90, 80, 80, 80

Flat bench dumbbell flyes: 4 sets of 8 with 50

Workout 42 (Biceps)

Heavy barbell curls: 4 sets of 6–8 with 145

Standing dumbbell alternating curls: 4 sets of 8 with 45, 45, 40, 35

Workout 43 (Back)

Superset wide-grip front pulldowns (5 sets of 10 reps with 160) to standing cable straight-bar, arms-locked front pulldowns/pullovers (5 sets of 10 with 90)

Close-grip front pulldowns: 3 sets of 10 with 130

T-bar rows: 5 sets of 8 with five 35-pound plates

Seated cable rows: 4 sets of 10 with 170

Workout 44 (Chest)

Dumbbell incline presses: 6 sets of 10 with 110; 6 sets with 100; 6 sets with 90; 6 sets with 80; 6 sets with 70; 6 sets with 60

Dumbbell incline flyes: 5 sets of 8 with 50

Dips: 4 sets of 10

Workout 45 (Shoulders)

Seated wide-grip barbell behind-the-neck presses: 8 sets of 6–8 reps with 145 for 6 sets, 125 for 2 sets

Standing dumbbell side laterals: 5 sets of 10 reps with 40, 40, 35, 30, 25

Workout 46 (Biceps/Triceps)

Seated dumbbell French presses (95) to seated Scott bench EZ-bar curls s(100): 5 supersets of 10

Workout 47 (Triceps/Biceps)

Lying EZ-bar French presses (100) to seated dumbbell alternating curls (45): 4 supersets of 8–10

Workout 48 (Legs)

Leg curls: 6 sets of 10–12 with 60 down to 30

Squats: 6 sets of 6–8 with 135, 8 reps with 225, 8 reps with 325, 4 reps with 415, 6 reps with 375, 15 reps with 325

Hack squats: 4 sets of 8–10 with 200

Leg extensions: 4 sets of 10–12 from 100 to 150

Superset machine standing calf raises (5 sets of 10–12 with 380) to bodyweight-only standing calf raises (5 sets of 15)

Workout 49 (Biceps)

Seated 45-degree dumbbell curls: 5 sets of 6–8 reps (35, 55, 60, 50, 45)

Seated dumbbell concentration curls: 5 sets of 15–20 with 35

Barbell Scott bench curls: 5 sets of limit with 70

Workout 50 (Chest)

Dumbbell incline presses: 5 sets of 8–12 with 60, 12 reps with 110, 8 reps with 100, 7 reps with 90, 6 reps with 80

Dumbbell incline flyes: 5 sets of 8 with 60 down to 45

Superset machine flat bench presses (160) to dips (to limit): 3 supersets

Workout 51 (Back)

Superset wide-grip chin-ups to straight stirrup-bar machine pulldowns (160 down to 130): 5 supersets of 8–10

Superset dumbbell pullovers (70) to seated cable rows (160): 5 supersets of 10–12

29

The Weak-Link Workouts

We all have certain body groups and muscles that are weaker than others, and those weaker muscles can hold us back from reaching our training goals. As they say, you're only as strong as your weakest link. Once you do this workout, those weak links may be a thing of the past.

You're going to use a type of training called dead stops. Many of the world's best strength athletes have used dead stops for years and have watched their progress skyrocket as a result. Weak-link dead-stop training means training the weakest point in any given exercise—that is, the part of the exercise you find the toughest. I suggest doing dead-stop and power-rack training once every two weeks.

Following are some great weak-link dead-stop workouts for every bodypart.

Legs: Squat
Use a power rack. Adjust the rack pins and do sets of quarter- and half-range movements. Without using the power rack, do a regular squat, but stop each rep at the bottom position for 2 seconds, then come back up and repeat. These dead stops will give you incredible power from the bottom position.

Quads–Inner Thighs: Leg Press with Feet Wide and Pointed Out
Use a weight that is about twice your bodyweight. Keep your feet wide on the platform and pointed outward. Always keep your knees in a straight line over your big toes while doing the reps.

Stay tight in the seat and don't allow your glutes to lift up and out of the seat when your legs and the platform come down. Come down as far as you can and stop at the point where you feel your glutes starting to rise up.

The feet and legs need to stay wide from start to finish in order to hit all the muscles you want to hit.

Lower Back/Hamstrings: Stiff-Legged Deadlift (Barbell or Dumbbell)
Do quarter- to half-range movements from starting position to half-lockout.

Squat (a)

Squat (b)

Squat with heels raised (a)

Squat with heels raised (b)

Leg press with feet wide and pointed out (a)

Leg press with feet wide and pointed out (b)

Deadlift (a)

Deadlift (b)

Then do another set of half- to full-lockout reps. Do dead stops at the bottom of the movement, too.

Hamstrings: Leg Curl (Lying, Seated, or Standing)
Do quarter- to half-range movements from starting position to half-lockout. When you have completed that, do

another set of half-lockout to full-lockout reps.

Calves: Calf Raise (Seated, Standing, or Donkey)
Do quarter- to half-range movements from starting position to half-lockout. Then do another set of half- to full-lockout reps.

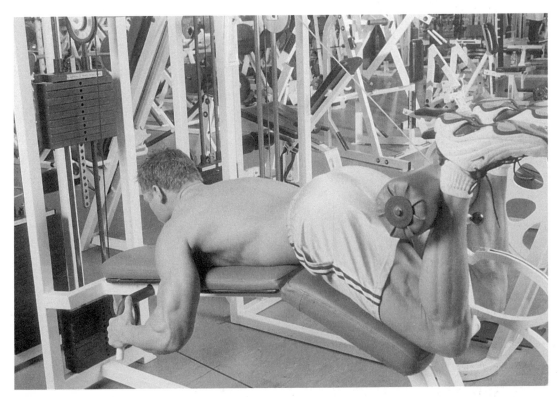

Leg curl (a)

Leg curl (b)

Seated calf raise (a)

Seated calf raise (b)

Calves: Leg Press Toe Raise

Place the balls of your feet on the bottom edge of the platform. Keep the weight pins/safety stops secured throughout this set. Keep your knees together and locked. Move only the toes and ankles—nothing else. Slowly lower the platform until you really feel it stretch your calves. You should feel it in the calves and up higher behind the knees and lower hamstrings. Hold the lowered position for 1 to 2 seconds, then toe press the platform up until your calves are fully extended. Do more than 20 reps per set.

Chest: Smith Machine or Power Rack Barbell Press

Set the pins in the power rack to allow only quarter- and half-range movements. On the Smith machine, do 2- to

Leg press toe raise

Smith machine or power rack barbell press (a)

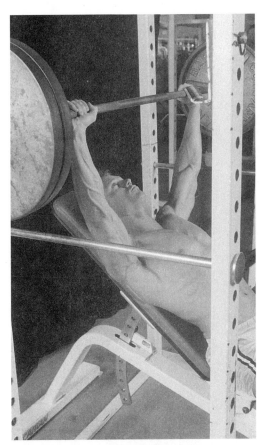

Smith machine or power rack barbell press (b)

3-second dead stops at the bottom of the exercise.

Traps: Barbell Shrug in Power Rack
Set the rack pins high enough that when you grab the barbell that's resting on top of the pins you won't have to bend over to pick it up. That is, place the barbell high enough so that with your arms straight down and elbows locked, you can grab the weight and then shrug it up a few inches then back down on top of the pins.

Back: Deadlift in Power Rack
Set the pins lower than you did for the shrug, at about knee level. Set the pins a few inches higher if you'd like to do quarter-range reps. Setting the pins at knee level will allow you to do half-range reps and will really help strengthen your erectors, which will help strengthen your legs because your lower back (the support column that holds the weight) will now be much stronger.

Barbell shrug in power rack (a)

Barbell shrug in power rack (b)

Deadlift in power rack (a)

Deadlift in power rack (b)

Shoulders: Barbell Press with Smith Machine or Power Rack

The 4 to 6 inches before you lock your arms in the barbell press is the strongest power range for the triceps, and doing quarter- and half-range movements will help build strength and power here. Yet for many people who do full-range rep training, it's at the lowest point of the movement—where the weight is at the bottom and you need to power it up—that they are weakest and need the most help.

I suggest doing power starts from this position: Allow the weight to come all the way down and let it rest for a few seconds in that bottom dead-stop position, then press it back up and repeat. This takes the momentum and cheat out of the exercise because it essentially becomes two separate exercises: from the top to the bottom, then stop; from the bottom to the top, then stop.

Biceps: Barbell Power Rack Curl

Set the power rack pins so that the barbell is positioned in the halfway point of the regular full-range barbell curl. At this, the starting point of the exercise, your forearms will be around the lower chest/stomach area and parallel with the floor. From here, curl the weight up until the biceps are fully

Barbell press with Smith machine or power rack (a)

Barbell press with Smith machine or power rack (b)

Barbell power rack curl (a)

Barbell power rack curl (b)

Barbell power rack curl (c)

contracted. Don't allow the weight to come too far back toward your shoulders because this will take the stress off the biceps.

Slowly lower the weight and repeat. For variety, do a few partial reps, curling the weight up just a few inches and then bringing it back down again.

Triceps: Flat Bench Barbell Press in Power Rack with Close Grip

Place the pins in a power rack so that you can bench press a barbell only about 3 to 6 inches above you. These 3 to 6 inches before your arms are fully locked are the strongest range for the triceps. Strengthening your triceps in this range of motion will help make

Flat bench barbell press in power rack with close grip (a)

Flat bench barbell press in power rack with close grip (b)

them stronger for all ranges of motion. I suggest experimenting with different hand spacings. Try shoulder width to narrow (6 to 8 inches apart). Feel which one hits you the best. Many people have found that the closer the grip, the more they feel it in the triceps, and the wider the grip, the more they feel it in the chest.

Abs: Crunch

The crunch is still one of the best ab exercises around. Remember, the key to making the crunch a great ab toner is to keep constant tension on the abs by doing nonstop reps and using a short range of motion. Keep the head and neck up and off the floor or bench throughout the set. No letting those

Crunch (a)

Crunch (b)

abs rest! I like keeping my feet and legs up off the floor and knees bent back toward my upper body. Do a set of 30 to 60 nonstop reps. You may even want to do a third of your reps with more emphasis on your left side, a third of the reps with emphasis on the right side, and the remaining third straight on.

RESEARCH UPDATE:
Burn More Calories the Easy Way

New research has added to the growing body of evidence showing that weight training is just as important as aerobic exercise in the fight against fat. Researchers at Johns Hopkins and Arizona State University found that after women did a series of resistance exercises involving weights, the number of calories they burned was raised for up to two hours after the workout.*

According to lead author Carol A. Binzen, "women who want to lose weight typically do aerobic exercises to raise their heart rate, thinking that's how they can burn the most calories." Binzen adds, "to get the maximum benefit, women need a combination of cardiovascular workouts and resistance training. Resistance training could have a more lasting effect on metabolism than aerobic exercise. It burns fat and increases muscle mass."

Researchers followed a group of 12 women aged 24 to 34 who train regularly with weights. On day one, the women performed 3 sets each of 10 reps of the following exercises:

- Chest press
- Shoulder press
- Leg extension
- Leg press
- Seated row
- Lat pulldown
- Arm curl
- Triceps extension
- Crunch

On another day, they sat still and watched a movie.

The research team compared the number of total calories and fat calories burned for up to two hours after exercise and while the subjects watched the movie. After completing the resistance training workout, the women burned 155 calories, compared with only 50 calories while watching the movie.

Moreover, 90 minutes *after* training with weights, the women were still burning more fat calories. "It might not seem like the exercises burned many more calories, but up to two hours after their workout, the women continued to have elevated metabolism as compared to when they watched the movie," Binzen says. "We studied regular women, not super fitness enthusiasts," she adds, "so these results may apply to most moderately active women."

---

* Binzen, C. A., P. D. Swan, and M. M. Manore. "Postexercise Oxygen Consumption and Substrate Use After Resistance Exercise in Women." *Medicine and Science in Sports and Exercise* 33 (2001): 932–38.

30

Leg Bodypart Specialization: Three Problem Areas for Both Women and Men

Many of you have written to me asking for specific help on changing the shape and look of your legs. Some of you have problems with outer thighs, some with inner thighs, and others with glutes. While genetics play a big role in the appearance of your body, there are some terrific exercises you can do that, if done in specific ways, will target those problem areas directly and give you great results.

GLUTES

You'll find lots of exercises and machines that will work the glutes, but people I've helped have always gotten great results from doing these exercises.

Squat
You already know about doing squats for the quads, but there is a little trick you can do that will shift the exercise emphasis to the glutes: simply lean the upper body forward slightly as you do

Squat with legs together

Squat with wide stance

the reps. Keeping the upper body erect seems to shift the exercise emphasis to the upper legs, but bending slightly forward gives emphasis to the glutes. Try these tips, too:

- Keep your feet firmly on the floor without having the heels elevated. Having heels elevated shifts the exercise emphasis to the quads, especially lower quads, depending on the elevation.
- The depth of your reps affects how much of the glute will be worked. Experiment and determine where you feel it most. Many people find that the lower they go—even slightly below parallel—the more they feel it hit the glutes.
- To vary the exercise, you can use a wide stance or have your legs together.

- Try a combination of low and high reps, from 6 to 25, and do 2 to 4 sets. You don't need to do these again just for glutes if you make this one of your main leg exercises.

Wide-Stance Deadlift

This is executed in the same way as a regular deadlift, only your hand and leg positions are different. Place your feet wider than shoulder-width apart with the toes pointed slightly outward and toward the inside of the weight plates. Take either a combination (one hand over, one hand under) grip or overhand grip about 6 to 8 inches apart on the middle of the bar. Keep your legs bent, bar close to your shins, upper body erect, and head up and looking forward.

Keeping your arms locked, drive the weight up with your legs. If need be, the upper body will lock into a straight vertical position at the end of the movement. Make the legs do the majority of the work. Do 3 to 4 sets of 5 to 7 reps.

Dumbbell Deadlift Between Legs

Do this exercise in the same manner as the wide-stance deadlift, but use one dumbbell instead of a barbell. Use the same body position as the wide-stance deadlift.

With both hands, hold a dumbbell between your legs. Keep your arms locked and both hands wrapped around the middle of the dumbbell knurling (the rough edge on the inside part of bar). Keep your upper torso erect and let the legs do the work. Do 3 to 4 sets of 12 to 16 nonstop reps.

Dumbbell Walking Lunge

Hold a dumbbell in each hand and keep the weights close to your body throughout the movement. Keep the upper body erect from start to finish. Do lunges in this sequence: one leg

Wide-stance deadlift (a)

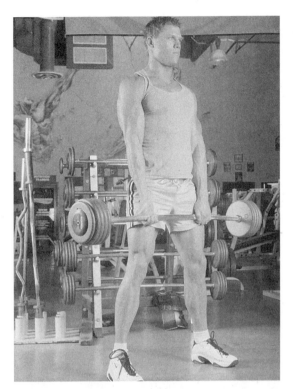

Wide-stance deadlift (b)

Dumbbell deadlift between legs (a)

Dumbbell deadlift between legs (b)

Dumbbell walking lunge (a)

Dumbbell walking lunge (b)

Dumbbell walking lunge (c)

steps forward, then the other leg kneels down; the first leg comes up and steps forward, then the opposite leg kneels down. Use straight-line steps and bring the knee directly over the foot that steps forward. On the leg that kneels down, keep the upper leg in a straight line under the upper torso. Don't allow the kneeling leg's knee to touch the floor. Take big steps forward. The bigger the step, the more you'll feel it hit the glutes. Do 3 to 4 sets of 15 to 20 steps for each leg.

Barbell/Smith Machine Stationary Lunge

Use the same leg position as the dumbbell walking lunge, but use a barbell or Smith machine. And instead of walking forward, you'll stay in one position and move only one leg back and forth at a time.

Keep the upper body and kneeling leg in a vertical upright position. Lunge forward only as far as you can go while keeping the upper body and kneeling leg in this straight up-and-down position. Do all your reps for

one leg before changing legs and doing the other side. Do 3 to 4 sets of 13 to 19 nonstop reps.

INNER THIGHS

Wide-Stance Ballet Squat

The Smith machine is much easier to use for this exercise because a lot of the movement depends on balance. Stand as you would when doing a regular squat. Keep the bar up high on your traps/lower neck. Space your legs wide and turn your feet out as far as possible. Try to keep your legs and feet as directly under the bar as you can. Your knees should travel in a straight line over the big toes from start to finish. Bend the knees and descend until the legs are about 3 to 4 inches above parallel. Return to the start position and do 3 to 4 sets of 11 to 16 reps.

Wide-Stance Leg Press

The wider the foot position, the more you'll feel it in the inner thighs. Do

Barbell/Smith machine stationary lunge (a)

Barbell/Smith machine stationary lunge (b)

Barbell/Smith machine stationary lunge (c)

Wide-stance ballet squat (a)

Wide-stance ballet squat (b)

Wide-stance leg press (a)

Wide-stance leg press (b)

these the same way you'd do your favorite leg press, only keep the feet wide apart and toes pointed outward and placed high on the foot platform. The farther you allow the platform/ weights to come down, the more you'll feel it work the inner thighs. Go for nonstop reps to keep the inner thighs burning. Do 3 to 4 sets of 15 to 25 reps.

Wide-Stance Hack Squat (Barbell or Machine)

Use a barbell or hack squat machine for this exercise. If you use the machine (as illustrated) try different foot positions (such as wide or narrow) to hit different areas on the quads. With a barbell, elevate your heels on

a 1- to 2-inch block or weight plates. Stand with feet about shoulder-width apart, toes turned slightly outward. Hold the barbell directly under and against the glutes/upper legs through- out the entire exercise. Keep the arms locked and the upper body erect and descend until the legs are a few inches above parallel. Do 3 to 4 sets of 10 to 13 reps.

Seated Double Cable Squeeze

Place a stool or flat bench in the middle of two low-pulley stacks and sit on the stool or at the end of the bench. With each hand, grab a stirrup- style cable handle attached to the low pulleys. Spread your legs, but keep your heels together and off the floor.

Wide-stance hack squat (a)

Wide-stance hack squat (b)

Seated double cable squeeze (a)

Seated double cable squeeze (b)

Only the balls of your feet should touch the floor. While holding the handles, lock your arms and bring them inside your legs so they are resting against the insides of your thighs. Keeping your upper torso erect and using only your legs and not your arms, squeeze your legs together until your arms touch each other. Slowly allow the legs to spread out again. Do 3 to 4 sets of 13 to 18 nonstop reps.

OUTER THIGHS

Squat

Here's a little trick to remember whenever you work legs: by simply changing foot position, you change where the exercise will hit the muscle. Keeping your feet wide hits the inner thighs; keeping feet together hits the outer

thighs. So keeping your feet together during a squat is a great way to work your outer thighs.

For one set, elevate your heels on a block or a pair of 25-pound plates. On the next set, use no heel elevation. What way do you feel it most? Where did you feel the differences?

Use nonstop near-lockout reps. The trick is to keep the legs constantly burning, and you do that by stopping each rep about three-quarters of the way at the top and then going back down again for the next rep. Do 3 to 4 sets of 15 to 25 nonstop three-quarters reps.

Leg Press with Feet Together

Here is another exercise with feet together to hit those outer thighs. Do one set with feet high on the platform, one set with feet in the middle of the

Squat (a)

Squat (b)

Squat with feet together (a)

Squat with feet together (b)

Leg press with feet together (a)

Leg press with feet together (b)

platform, and one set with feet low on the platform. How did each set feel? Where did you feel it?

Change seat position, too. On one set, have the seat all the way declined. On another set, raise the seat a few notches. Keep your feet in the same position when moving the seat. You want to find out whether there are any differences in the way you feel the exercise simply by adjusting body position from moving the seat. Once you've determined that, then add changing your foot position on the

platform and find the combination where you feel it best. Do 3 to 4 sets of 18 to 22 nonstop three-quarters reps.

Hack Squat with Knees Together

Use the same foot positions as for the leg press with feet together. On one set, keep your upper body against the hack squat back pad. Next set, lift your glutes and lower back off the back pad so that your legs come farther forward over the knees. Which way do you feel it best? Do 3 to 4 sets of 16 to 20 nonstop three-quarters reps.

Hack squat with knees together (a)

Hack squat with knees together (b)

31

Pre- and Post-Weight Training Cardio Workouts

Differing views abound regarding what are the best cardiovascular exercises and how much cardio work is ideal. One size doesn't fit all when it comes to cardio. Someone wanting to run long distances will train much differently from the powerlifter looking to set a world record.

I think bodybuilders are somewhere in between. While too much cardio can tire them out and tap into recuperative and muscle-building capacities, the right amount of cardio will help keep them leaner and improve endurance. Truth be told, there are lots of people who work out and do cardio just so they can eat whatever they want without worrying about it affecting their appearance.

After finding the right amount of cardio to do, you must decide when to do it: Before the workout? After the workout? In the middle of the workout? Some prefer to do cardio before working out because it gets the heart pumping, the blood flowing, and the body moving and warmed up. Others like doing it after the workout because

they feel like they can keep more of their strength for the weights and they think cardio is a nice finish to a good workout. A few people will do cardio between bodyparts or even do it while they're working out by holding dumbbells in their hands and exercising as they walk on the treadmill, step on the stairclimber, or pedal the bike. You have many options. It's all about what feels best to you.

Personally, I find myself going in spurts with cardio training. At certain times in the year I'll hit the cardio hard and lighten up on the weights. At other times I minimize the direct cardio work but train quickly with almost no rest between sets. Regardless of the time of year when I'm training, I always do one thing that has gotten me into good cardio condition and has kept me there—train quickly and with minimal rest.

This kind of training is tough. Your body wants to rest after a tough set. There's a trade-off to training this way: you'll be giving up maximum poundages for slightly lighter weights,

RESEARCH UPDATE:
Aerobic Fitness

If you want to get fit but don't have time for long bouts of exercise, researchers from Stanford University have some good news.* An eight-week study of healthy men aged 45 to 58 showed that just three 10-minute bouts of exercise each day improved aerobic fitness by more than 7 percent. Most people think that in order to get fit, you need to spend hours in the gym. However, this study shows that simply accumulating a certain amount of activity each week is enough to improve your fitness.

One of the main benefits for people who get fit is an increased capacity to burn fat.

The flow of blood in a "fit" muscle is greater than that in an "unfit" muscle. Moreover, there's also a rise in the activity of enzymes responsible for burning fat. In other words, if they both trained at the same relative intensity, a trained individual would use more fat calories for fuel than an untrained individual.

That said, it's important to point out that people who get fit aren't always lean. In fact, researchers from the Cooper Institute in Dallas and the University of Houston have shown that lean men benefit from increased longevity only if they're physically fit. Moreover, overweight men who get fit are *less likely* to die from cardiovascular disease than lean men who are unfit. In short, it appears that being fit can

counter some of the health risks linked to excess body fat.

Not only can short bouts of exercise help to improve your fitness and promote weight loss, they also make it more likely you'll stick to your program. You see, the real secret to making exercise a lifelong habit is to set activity goals that are realistic, not ridiculous. The mistake most people make is to take an all-or-nothing approach. If they can't do everything they think they should be doing, they end up doing nothing. However, as this study shows, even a few short bouts of exercise (such as brisk walking or cycling) performed daily *will* make a difference in your fitness level.

* DeBusk, R. F., U. Stenestrand, M. Sheehan, and W. L. Haskell. "Training Effects of Long Versus Short Bouts of Exercise in Healthy Subjects." *American Journal of Cardiology* 65 (1990): 1010–13.

but you'll be gaining much better conditioning.

Two things surprised me about training this way. The first was when I was living in Idaho and went snowshoeing for the first time. The snow was knee deep, yet I was easily able to do 60 minutes with a sustained heart rate of 145 to 180 beats per minute. I hadn't done specific cardio conditioning prior to getting out in the snow; I simply had weight trained. But I had trained with 10 to 30 seconds of rest between sets and not more than a minute's rest between bodyparts (just enough to get a drink).

The other wonderfully surprising thing was that if I got on a treadmill after doing no cardio training for months (I was always doing high- to moderate-intensity workouts with minimal rest) I'd be able to train at the

levels where I had previously cardio trained months earlier, and with the same amount of ease and workout intensity.

So what type of cardio exercise should you do, and how long should you do it? I like using only a handful of pieces of cardio equipment. Power walking—either on the treadmill or outside—is my favorite. I've found that hitting the cardio before (especially good for warming up legs before leg workouts) or after working out, anywhere from 12 to 25 minutes, will work great for the *Bodybuilding 201* athlete who's also hitting the weights hard.

Power Walk (Treadmill)
Always take big, long strides to work more hamstring, calf, and glute muscles and make the exercise more intense and effective. Keep the upper

body erect and swing those arms back and forth with each step in a natural motion. Take deep breaths with each step and put some power behind your steps. You're bound for great results if you follow this 12-minute power walking treadmill workout. Adjust your times as needed.

- Begin with the treadmill at 0 degrees of elevation (flat) and increase the speed to 3.5 to 3.7 miles per hour (mph).
- Take long strides with your upper torso and head erect. Look forward.
- With each stride, swing your arms up and out in front of and behind you in rhythm. Think big movements for the arms and legs.

- At the 2-minute mark, raise the treadmill elevation to 3 to 5 degrees (depending on how easy or difficult it is) and increase the treadmill speed to 3.8 to 4.0 mph.
- At the 6-minute mark, raise the treadmill elevation to 7 to 10 degrees (depending on how easy or difficult it is) and keep the treadmill speed between 3.8 and 4.0 mph.
- At the 10-minute mark, lower the treadmill elevation to 5 degrees and reduce the speed to 3.5 mph.
- At the 11-minute mark, lower the treadmill to 0-degree elevation (completely flat) and reduce the speed to 3.0 mph.
- At the 12-minute mark, stop and get off; you're finished.

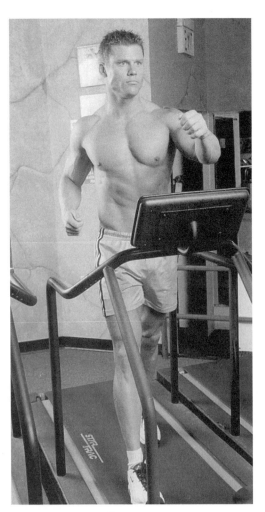

Power walk (treadmill) (a)

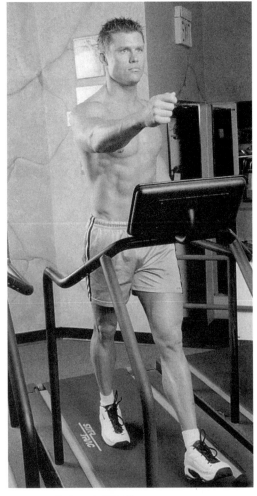

Power walk (treadmill) (b)

Stairclimber

When working out on the stairclimber, keep your body straight up and down—none of this leaning over or turning your hands and gripping the rails. Touch the rails only if you must to regain your upper-body balance. Your hands and arms should be free throughout the exercise. As you step, move your arms just as you would if you were walking up a flight of stairs.

Keep only the balls of your feet on the back of the stepper. As each step goes down, let your heel come all the way down for a good stretch; then as the step comes up, let your heel come all the way up as high as possible to get a good calf contraction. These two things turn the stairclimber machine into a fabulous calf exercise.

To get the most from the exercise for your glutes, hamstrings, and legs, be sure to take big, full steps all the way up and all the way down. Big strides produce big results.

Set the exercise program to manual—just like on the treadmill. After a 1-minute warm-up of moderate resistance, increase the resistance until you find just the right step cadence that allows you to come all the way down without going too fast or too slow. With so many different stairclimber machines out there, it's difficult for me to tell you where this will be, but you'll quickly find just the perfect spot for you.

Stairclimber (a)

Stairclimber (b)

If you're looking for a terrific stairclimber workout, try this quick 12-minute workout. Adjust your times as needed.

- Place the balls of your feet on the edge of the steps.
- Keep your upper body erect. *No bending over!*
- Place your hands over the rails with your palms down; do not use a reverse grip with your palms turned away from you.
- Use the manual program.
- Begin stepping. Take full, complete steps—none of this limited-motion, quick-stepping stuff. Go for long strides.
- As you find your rhythm, begin to loosen your grip on the rails until you can step without holding on to anything.
- Concentrate on taking long strides and moving your arms back and forth and up and down until you are in a groove.
- Allow each step to go all the way up so that you feel it in your glutes, hamstrings, and quads and all the way down so that you feel the big stretch and contraction in your calves. If you do it right, this is an incredible calf shaper.
- Don't be concerned about speed. Go for full strides up and down without stopping. Speed will come as you become better conditioned and accustomed to doing this exercise.
- At the 12-minute mark, stop and get off; you're finished.
- Stretch all body groups worked, with additional emphasis on any areas you choose.

Stationary Bike

Adjust the seat high enough so that when the pedal is at the bottom of the stroke your knee will have only a slight bend. Set the exercise program to manual, begin pedaling, and set the resistance level to 2. Pedal at the rate of 80 revolutions per minute (rpm) for 1 minute at level 2. At the 2-minute mark, change the level of resistance to 3 until the 3-minute mark, then to level 4. At the 4-minute mark move to level 5, and so on until you've reached a level where it's tough for you to maintain 80 rpm. Once you find that level, reduce it by one or two levels and keep your bike cardio work there until you've done 15 to 20 minutes of pedaling. Be sure to always maintain at least 80 rpm.

If you like to mix things up and wouldn't mind sitting and reading while you cardio your way to awesomeness, then the bike is calling your name. Here's a cool little 12-minute workout that'll work wonders. Adjust your times accordingly.

- Elevate the seat so that when the pedal is down at the lowest position of the stroke, there's a slight bend to your knee.
- Begin pedaling and set the program for manual training.
- Begin the program at level 2 and maintain 80 to 92 rpm for 2 minutes.
- At the 2-minute mark, increase the level to 4 and maintain 80 to 85 rpm.
- At the 5-minute mark, increase the level to 6 and maintain 80 rpm.
- At the 8-minute mark, decrease the level to 3 and maintain 95 to 100 rpm.
- At the 10-minute mark, decrease the level to 2 and maintain 90 to 95 rpm.
- At the 11-minute mark, decrease the level to 1 and maintain 75 to 80 rpm.
- At the 12-minute mark, stop and get off; you're finished.

Stationary bike

Bodybuilding 201 is all about one thing: you. You've decided to take your body and training to the next level, and this book is all about your success. So go as far as you can and you'll be smiling at the results. Of this I am sure.

As you reach new goals and become what you're capable of being, I want to know how you did it. I want to hear about how you changed your body, thinking, and life using tips from *Bodybuilding 201*. I also want to know about anything else you've found helpful.

For my next book, I'd like to do something a bit different and include the best stories from men and women all over the world who changed how they look and feel, along with their "real world" tips about how anyone can do the same.

That's why I want you to E-mail me and tell me your story—so I can share it with the world. I know you've got lots to say and an inspiring story to tell, so get writing and E-mail it to me at www.robertwolff.com. Who knows what great things could happen!

It's been said that we are only as strong as our weakest link. While our muscles may be strong, our knees, elbows, shoulders, and ankles—where so much of the force of our weight exercise is directed—aren't.

Let's face it: the human body wasn't designed to squat 700 pounds, bench press 400, shoulder press 225, or do sports that twist knees and ankles. That's why you need to exercise intelligently and listen to your body and treat it well. It's all about maximizing gain and minimizing pain (the debilitating kind).

You may say, "Yeah, great. Thanks for telling me all this now. So, what if I've been injured? What kind of treatment and rehab options do I have?" Glad you asked. Dr. Jeffrey Halbrecht will see you now.

IF YOU'VE INJURED YOUR SHOULDER

Rotator Cuff Injury

The rotator cuff is a group of four muscles and their tendon attachments that surround the shoulder joint. These tendons attach to the ball of the shoulder (humeral head) and act as the inner "ball bearing" stabilizers of the joint. The rotator cuff needs to function properly for the outer layer of large muscles to do their job.

The muscles that constitute the rotator cuff are the supraspinatus, which elevates the shoulder; the subscapularis, which internally rotates the shoulder; and the infraspinatus and teres minor, which externally rotate the shoulder. The supraspinatus is the one most commonly involved in injury.

Pinching, or impingement, of the rotator cuff can occur against the overlying bone, called the acromion. This can occur due to a spur on the acromion, or a thickening or curvature of this bone that rubs against the tendon. The result is inflammation of the tendon (rotator cuff tendinitis) and its adjacent lubricating sac, the bursa (bursitis).

If the impingement persists for extended periods, actual tearing of the rotator cuff tendons may occur. X-rays are usually necessary to confirm the presence of a special spur. Tearing of the tendon is best detected with a special type of x-ray called an MRI (magnetic resonance imaging).

Symptoms: Aching pain on the side of the upper arm is the most common complaint. Pain is often worse at night and with overhead arm motions. Throwing, tennis, and weightlifting are particularly painful. There may be some clicking in the shoulder due to thickening of the inflamed bursa.

Weakness suggests that the rotator cuff may be torn.

Treatment Options: Seventy percent of patients improve with nonsurgical care. Initial treatment involves anti-inflammatory medication, ice, and avoiding over-the-shoulder reaching and lifting activities. In the very acute painful phase, exercises are avoided. When pain subsides somewhat, rotator cuff exercises are prescribed.

The primary goal of the exercises is to work the uninjured portion of the rotator cuff. This is accomplished by emphasizing internal and external rotation exercises using elastic tubing. Scapula stabilizers are also strengthened.

Deep tissue work by a physical therapist can help relieve associated spasm. Isolated strengthening of the most commonly injured supraspinatus tendon should be avoided. If there is no response to this treatment program, an injection of cortisone is the next step. Cortisone is a strong anti-inflammatory medication that, when used appropriately and sparingly, is safe and can be dramatically beneficial.

Surgery: If there is no response to conservative care for a minimum of three months, surgery becomes an option. The purpose of the surgery is to remove the bone spur from the acromion. This surgery is performed arthroscopically using three small punctures in the shoulder. If the tendon is found to be torn, it is repaired arthroscopically, avoiding an incision in most cases. All surgery is performed on an outpatient basis and typically takes one hour.

Aftercare: Following surgery, a sling is worn for one day and range-of-motion exercises are begun. The amount of activity allowed depends on the severity of the injury to the rotator cuff.

Prognosis: Ninety percent of patients achieve a good to excellent result following surgery and are able to return to full activities.

Weightlifting: Weightlifting is a common cause of rotator cuff injuries. Many lifting exercises can be modified so as to protect the rotator cuff and avoid reinjury. The basic concept is to avoid positions that will impinge the tendons.

A practical approach is to draw an imaginary box that extends from your chin to your hips and is shoulder width. Modify your lifting program so that your hands stay within this box. For example, do pulldowns in front of your body rather than behind your head. Avoid flyes; instead, use the Nautilus pec machine with the range of motion restricted to avoid excessive hyperextension of the shoulder. Do the bench press in a limited arc so that your elbows never break the imaginary plane (don't let the elbows extend behind your body). Do pull-ups and similar exercises with your palms toward your face. This places your shoulders in external rotation, moving the most vulnerable portion of the rotator cuff out of the way of the acromion.

Internal Impingement (Thrower's Shoulder)

Throwing athletes, tennis players, volleyball players, and other athletes who perform lots of over-the-shoulder movements often suffer from shoulder pain. New studies suggest that a common cause of this pain may be a newly described entity called internal impingement. This is the internal pinching of the underside of the rotator cuff tendon against the glenoid, the socket joint of the shoulder. This pinching occurs when the arm is placed all the way back into the throwing position. Over time, this pinching can lead to tearing of the tendon and shoulder pain.

Symptoms and Diagnosis: The diagnosis is often difficult to make and usually requires evaluation by a shoulder expert. The patient usually complains of posterior pain (backside of the shoulder) that is aggravated when throwing. There is usually no associated instability or significant weakness. Examination by a physician will reveal a positive relocation test. MRI may be useful if performed with dye enhancement with the arm in the throwing position. Final confirmation of the diagnosis is often made only at the time of surgery.

Treatment Options: Most athletes will respond to rehabilitation exercises to strengthen the rotator cuff and the scapula. In persistent cases, arthroscopic surgery can be very helpful in confirming the diagnosis and debriding, or removing, the torn portion of the rotator cuff tendon. Recovery is usually remarkably quick following this particular surgery, with a return to throwing sports in several weeks.

Aftercare: Surgery is performed on an outpatient basis. All dressings and the sling are removed after one day and physical therapy begins immediately.

Prognosis: Excellent results can be achieved with arthroscopic management, and most athletes return to their preinjury level of sports participation.

AC Joint Separation

The acromioclavicular (AC) joint is the junction of the collarbone (clavicle) and the shoulder. Separation of the AC joint occurs with a fall on the shoulder that tears the ligaments that stabilize the clavicle. This results in elevation of the clavicle, creating a prominent bump on the top of the shoulder. Complete tearing of the ligaments is called a grade 3 injury.

Treatment Options: Most AC separations can be treated with a sling for a few weeks to control pain and allow healing. The clavicle will always remain elevated, but function will return to normal levels in over 90 percent of cases. For very severe separations, or occasionally for a professional athlete, surgical repair may be recommended. For the majority of these injuries, however, conservative treatment is recommended.

AC Arthritis

Degeneration of the acromioclavicular joint is common in weightlifters and in laborers, and can be quite painful. Because of the proximity of the AC joint to the rotator cuff, patients with AC arthritis will often be misdiagnosed as having rotator cuff problems. With arthritis there will be tenderness directly over the AC joint and pain with movement of the arm across the chest to touch the opposite shoulder. Often the joint will be prominent with an overlying spur.

Treatment Options: Treatment involves the injection of cortisone, use of ice, activity modification, and occasionally surgery. Surgical treatment involves arthroscopically removing the arthritic portion of the clavicle.

Aftercare: Surgery is performed on an outpatient basis and takes one hour. The postsurgical sling and bandages are removed the day after surgery. Range-of-motion exercises and physical therapy begin immediately.

Prognosis: About 90 percent of patients will obtain excellent range of motion and be able to return to weightlifting and over-the-shoulder lifting activities. Complete recovery often takes several months.

Shoulder Instability

The shoulder is the most mobile joint in the body and is therefore the one most prone to instability. Types of instability include the following:

- *Subluxation*: Partial dislocation of the joint; the ball slides partially out of the socket but never truly dislocates
- *Dislocation*: Complete displacement of the ball out of the socket

  There are three different directions of shoulder instability:

- *Anterior*: The most common form (95 percent of all instability); the shoulder comes out the front.
- *Multidirectional*: All of the shoulder ligaments are loose and the joint is unstable in more than one direction. Typically the shoulder will be unstable in the front and downward, but a posterior direction may also be involved. This type of instability is sometimes seen in swimmers and other athletes who do many repetitive motions with their upper extremities.
- *Posterior*: The shoulder comes out the back. This type of instability is most rare and typically occurs with seizure disorders or unusual trauma.

Symptoms and Diagnosis: Patients with subtle forms of instability will only occasionally complain of a feeling of instability. More often the subluxation episodes cause pain or numbness in the arm. Diagnosis depends on a medical history and physical examination by a shoulder expert.

Cases of complete dislocation are easier to diagnose. Typically the patient will have had to go to an emer-

gency room to have the shoulder reduced, and an x-ray will confirm that the shoulder has come out of the socket. These patients complain primarily of instability, particularly with the arm in the overhead position.

Treatment Options: Treatment depends on the severity of the instability and the age of the patient. The younger the patient, the more likely the shoulder will dislocate repeatedly. Repeated dislocations can severely limit activities and are thought to lead to degeneration of the joint.

Studies have shown that immobilization and strengthening have minimal influence on the prognosis. The only way to predictably limit the risk of recurrent dislocation is surgery. Current recommendations are to repair the torn ligaments for recurrent dislocations and to consider surgery even for the first-time dislocation in the very young athlete.

Surgery: Surgical options include the following:

- *Arthroscopic Bankart repair*: Almost all types of instability can be treated arthroscopically. If the ligaments are completely torn, they can be reattached using small tacks placed arthroscopically without a need for an incision (Bankart repair). Current methods have been shown to provide approximately a 90 percent success rate in preventing dislocation.
- *Shrinkage capsulorraphy*: If the ligaments are stretched but not torn, there are several exciting new arthroscopic methods for tightening them. Sutures may be used to tighten the ligaments, or the ligaments may be heated, shrinking the tissue and causing the ligaments to tighten. Both methods are performed arthroscopically without incisions.

Aftercare: A sling is worn for three weeks. Early (i.e., the beginning stages of) range of motion begins. Over-the-shoulder reaching is limited for six weeks. Strengthening is progressive, including a slow return to throwing activities. A full return to contact sports is not allowed for six months.

Prognosis: Without surgical treatment most patients will continue to suffer episodes of instability. With surgery, 90 percent of patients will never dislocate again and will be able to return to all sports activities.

IF YOU'VE INJURED YOUR ELBOW

Tennis Elbow

Tendinitis of the elbow is often referred to as tennis elbow due to its common occurrence in tennis players. Actually, any sport or activity that requires gripping can cause this problem. Repetitive gripping or a sudden severe force, such as a backhand shot in tennis, can cause microscopic tearing of the tendons that attach on the outside of the elbow. The body's attempt to heal this tear results in the inflammation that causes tennis elbow.

Symptoms: People with tennis elbow report pain with gripping and lifting; often, even lifting a cup of coffee is painful.

Treatment Options: Nonoperative treatments include ice, stretching, avoiding gripping, using a tennis elbow strap, and anti-inflammatory medicine. Physical therapy is sometimes helpful for ultrasound, deep friction massage, and iontophoreses. Physical therapy helps promote blood flow, which in turn helps these healing modalities. Acupuncture is recommended in resistant cases.

Surgery is recommended in the most resistant cases after six months of failed nonoperative treatment. Traditional surgery releases the involved tendon and removes damaged tissue. A much less invasive technique that is done in the office under local anesthesia is a better option; patients are sent home with a bandage and begin to use the arm almost immediately.

Thrower's Elbow

Baseball players and other throwing athletes subject their elbows to tremendous stress. The throwing motion causes compression of the outside structures of the elbow and tension on the inside structures. Over time the compression leads to bone spurs and chips, and the tension leads to stretching of the ligaments. In severe cases, loose fragments (bodies) may form that need to be removed. If the ligaments stretch beyond a certain point, they may need to be tightened or reconstructed.

Ulnar Nerve Entrapment

The "funny bone" is actually not a bone but an exposed area where the ulnar nerve passes around the elbow. Anyone who has ever banged the funny bone knows how sensitive this nerve can be. This nerve may become chronically inflamed and entrapped in its tight passage around the elbow (the passage is called the cubital tunnel).

Symptoms: Patients report burning pain and tingling at the elbow and down the arm to the ring and pinky fingers.

Treatment Options: Nonoperative treatments include splinting, immobilization, rest, ice, and anti-inflammatory medicine. If symptoms fail to resolve with nonsurgical options, surgery is recommended to avoid permanent damage to the nerve. At surgery, the nerve is released from its tight passage

ELBOW ARTHROSCOPY

Although elbow arthroscopy is considered more complex than arthroscopy of many other joints due to the complicated structure of this joint and the location of many nerves and vessels surrounding the joint, this type of surgery has many advantages over open surgery, particularly at the elbow. Because of the complex nature of this joint, it is prone to becoming stiff after surgery. Arthroscopy allows surgery to be performed through tiny puncture holes, without any incisions. Postsurgical pain is greatly reduced, allowing earlier range of motion and less risk of stiffness, and external scarring is for the most part eliminated. For these reasons the use of arthroscopy in the elbow has become more common.

A list of elbow problems that may be treated arthroscopically follows:

- Loose bodies (fragments) in the joint
- Chondromalacia (cartilage damage)
- Elbow arthritis
- Osteochondritis dissecans
- Scar tissue
- Olecranon impingement (thrower's elbow)
- Tennis elbow

and relocated to a more protected area. Surgery is done as an outpatient procedure, and a splint is used for a few days, followed by range-of-motion and strengthening exercises.

Loose Bodies

If loose fragments are present in the elbow joint they can cause irreversible damage to the joint and must be removed. A loose body in the joint is like a pebble in a gear and will grind and damage the joint. These bodies are removed arthroscopically. In weight training, loose bodies can be caused by using too much weight, insufficient warm-up, and poor exercise form.

Symptoms: As with ulnar nerve entrapment, patients report burning pain and tingling at the elbow and down the arm to the ring and pinky fingers.

IF YOU'VE INJURED YOUR KNEE

Anterior Cruciate Ligament (ACL) Injury

The anterior cruciate ligament (ACL) is an important stabilizing ligament of the knee. It is located deep inside the knee joint and provides almost 90 percent of the stability to forward force on the joint. Injuries to this ligament are very common in aggressive sports such as skiing and basketball.

Injury to the ACL usually occurs with a sudden hyperextension or rotational force to the joint. The exact mechanism differs for different sports. Typically the injured athlete will hear or feel a "pop" and will have sudden onset of pain, instability, and swelling. If this occurs, the athlete should not attempt to continue playing and should seek medical attention.

Because the ACL is such an important stabilizer of the knee, injury to the ligament makes it difficult to participate in aggressive twisting sports. It should be emphasized that certain "straight-ahead" sports, such as bicycling, rollerblading, light jogging, and swimming, can be performed quite well with an injured ACL or without one altogether, should the ACL need to be removed. Twisting, cutting, and jumping sports are not recommended due to the risk of the knee giving way.

The knee is designed to work as a hinge, moving in one plane. With a torn ACL, there is increased play in the joint, allowing shearing forces across the cartilage surface and leading to progressive tearing of the cartilage disks (menisci) and breakdown of the joint surface. Over time, this break-down leads to degenerative arthritis.

Treatment Options: Treatment of ACL injuries has come a long way in the past 10 years. Today athletes have greater than a 90 percent chance of returning to their preinjury level of sports participation.

Conservative care is recommended for minor and partial tears of the ACL, or tears in which the knee is still within the accepted limits of stability (less than 3 millimeters of laxity). Nonsurgical treatment is also recommended for the patient who is willing to modify activity to nontwisting, less aggressive sports. Such athletes may begin an immediate specialized rehabilitation program and get a custom-fitted knee brace for use during sports activity.

Surgery for ACL injuries is extremely specialized and should be performed only by a surgeon who specializes in this type of injury. The techniques continue to change, and only someone on the cutting edge can hope to stay up with the latest technology. Your surgeon should perform *at least 50* of these operations a year. The current state-of-the-art recommendations include the following:

- The surgery should be entirely arthroscopic.
- Associated surgeries, such as meniscus repairs, should be done arthroscopically.
- Immediate weight bearing should be allowed following surgery.
- Accelerated rehabilitation is allowed (motion begins immediately).

Surgical options include the following:

- *Suture repair of the ACL:* This is rarely the best choice for an ACL injury but is recommended in certain rare situations when the ligament is torn off its attachment site but is still intact and not stretched out, or when it tears off with a fragment of bone. Studies have proved that in most situations repair is less likely to have a good outcome than a full reconstruction.
- *Reconstruction:* This means creating a new ligament out of a tendon from another location in the patient's knee or from cadaver tissue. There are three popular choices for the tissue:
  - Patella tendon (autograft): The most popular choice for this surgery, this involves taking a strip of the tendon from the front of the athlete's own knee (autograft). This technique has been used for the longest period of time in the largest number of patients and is considered the gold standard for ACL reconstruction. It allows healing in just four to six weeks. A minor disadvantage: this surgery requires taking tissue from the body, which may cause donor-site soreness in a small percentage of patients. However, this can be prevented by means of a unique method for harvesting the patella tendon graft.
  - Hamstrings: This newer method is gaining popularity. It is recommended for patients who are not candidates for patella tendon use. For some surgeons, this technique may result in a lower incidence of donor-site discomfort. One disadvantage: hamstring tendons do not come with bone attachments, and it takes the body 12 weeks to heal the hamstring graft (three times as long as the patella tendon). This means that in the early postopera-

tive period the graft is at risk for injury for a longer period of time.

- Allograft: This technique employs tissue from a cadaver. It is an attractive option in cases where multiple ligaments are injured and additional tissue is needed for surgery, or for revision cases where the patient's own patella tendon has already been used. The obvious advantage of this technique is that there's no need to take tissue from the patient's already injured knee. This may be a good idea in the older patient, whose own tissue may be weaker than the usually young donor. But this method has lost popularity recently because of some reports that an allograft is more likely to stretch and fail than an autograft. This is partly due to the weakening of the graft caused by irradiation performed to prevent disease transmission. Unfortunately, even after irradiating the donor graft tissue, the risk of transmitting disease still exists, although it is small.

- *ACL tightening (shrinkage):* We are currently performing a study using a new technique that tightens the partially torn or stretched ACL. (It may not be used for a completely torn ligament.) Surgery is done arthroscopically with no incisions. Recovery time is dramatically faster than with a reconstruction. So far, we have been impressed with the ability to tighten the ligament at the time of surgery (average 50 percent reduction in laxity). We are following these patients closely to determine whether the ligament will stretch.

Aftercare: Patients are sent home with a knee brace for the first day. Range-of-motion treatment begins as soon as the wound is checked. Early goals are to obtain range of motion and to reeducate the muscles. Weight bearing is begun immediately with crutches. The brace is used for three weeks or until the quadriceps are strong enough to support the limb. Crutches are discontinued after one to two weeks.

Patients begin stationary bicycling as soon as they can achieve 100 degrees of flexion and can get around on the pedal (usually two weeks). Outdoor bicycling and jogging are allowed at three months. Twisting, cutting, and jumping sports are delayed for six months because this is how long it takes for the graft to biologically heal. Prior to returning to sports, the patient is expected to have regained 90 to 95 percent of muscular strength.

Prognosis: ACL reconstruction is a highly successful operation. About 90 to 95 percent of patients can be expected to return to full sports participation within six months with aggressive rehabilitation.

Meniscus Damage

The meniscus is a circular-shaped disk of cartilage tissue that functions as a shock absorber between the bones of the knee. The meniscus is frequently damaged in twisting injuries or with repetitive impact over time. When the meniscus tears, a piece of cartilage can move in an abnormal way inside the joint, causing pain and swelling. Because cartilage has no blood supply, normal healing does not occur.

Treatment Options: New techniques allow the meniscus to be repaired arthroscopically, using sutures or small dissolving tacks, eliminating the need for an incision in many cases. When the torn meniscus cannot be repaired, the smallest possible amount of tissue is removed in order to preserve as much cushion for the joint as possible. In rare cases, where a large portion of

CHONDROCYTE IMPLANTATION

Younger patients with an isolated articular cartilage injury to the surface of the femur in the knee joint can benefit from one of the most exciting advances in the treatment of knee injuries. In chondrocyte implantation, cartilage cells are taken from the injured knee and cloned in the laboratory, then implanted back into the joint to regrow cartilage on the damaged surface. This technique was initiated in Sweden and has been available in the United States since 1995.

Results: Over a thousand patients have been treated worldwide with chondrocyte implantation. Current results indicate that patients can expect a 90 percent chance of successful treatment for isolated articular cartilage injuries of the femur.

Treatment Options: Cartilage tissue is removed arthroscopically from the injured knee and sent to a special laboratory where the cells are removed and cloned using specialized cell culturing techniques. The initial procedure to remove the cells is performed under local anesthesia and can be performed in the office. The cells are then implanted four weeks later.

Implantation of the cells is performed through an incision to expose the joint and to sew in a patch of tissue to cover the joint defect. The patch is taken from the lining of the adjacent bone. The cartilage cells are then implanted underneath the patch and the patch is sealed using a "glue" made from the patient's own blood serum.

Aftercare: Patients are placed into a passive motion machine for two weeks. Quadriceps contractions and leg raises are begun immediately. Weight bearing is not allowed for six weeks in order to protect the cell implant. After six weeks, weight bearing and a progressive strengthening and functional exercise program begins. Sports are delayed for six months to one year, to allow maturation of the cartilage.

Prognosis: We are currently collecting clinical data on all patients and are performing second-look arthroscopies on those who consent to it. To date, all the implantations have taken, and there have been no technical failures. Clinical results so far are in the 80 to 90 percent success range for good to excellent relief of symptoms. Additional studies are being performed to assess the physiological results. These include the use of bone scans and specialized MRI spectroscopy techniques. This data collection is ongoing; it will be three to five years before statistically significant data is available.

the meniscus has to be removed, current techniques allow transplantation of a new meniscus from a cadaver.

Aftercare: Surgery is done on an outpatient basis using arthroscopic techniques. Immediate weight bearing is allowed and crutches are used for 48 hours. Movement and modality treatment and physical therapy are started immediately. Bandages are removed after 24 hours and disposable adhesive bandages are applied. Stationary bicycling is allowed within a few days.

Prognosis: Results are 90 to 95 percent successful, with full return to sports at four to six weeks for most surgeries.

Complex repairs and transplants may take six months for full recovery.

IF YOU'VE INJURED YOUR PATELLA (KNEECAP)

The patella is a relatively small bone in the front of the knee that is embedded in the quadriceps (thigh muscle) tendon and acts to increase the biomechanical leverage of the quadriceps. The patella slides in a groove on the femur as the knee flexes and extends.

Because the patella "floats" within the substance of the quadriceps, proper tracking of this bone in the femoral groove depends on proper muscle balance to maintain a central position. Congenital anatomic factors, such as the shape of the patella, also influence this tracking.

Also, because of the location of the patella, it is subject to higher stresses than other joint surfaces. So, despite having a thicker cartilage lining than any other bone, it often begins to wear out before other parts of the knee.

Chondromalacia Patella

Chondromalacia patella refers to softening or breakdown of cartilage. It is one of the most common problems to affect the knee and is particularly common in running and jumping athletes. Chondromalacia begins as softening of the otherwise very resilient cartilage and proceeds to cracking and eventually complete loss of the cartilage lining beneath the patella.

Symptoms: Patients report pain in the front of the knee, crunching under the kneecap, and swelling in the knee. Symptoms increase with climbing stairs or sitting for long periods. Early on, symptoms may simply be mild aching in the area of the patella.

In later stages of chondromalacia, the cartilage surface of the patella becomes roughened as pieces of cartilage begin to break off. This roughened surface causes a crunching sound under the patella and can lead to swelling of the knee.

Treatment Options: Initial treatment focuses on physical therapy techniques for strengthening the muscles around the patella to balance the patella tracking and more evenly distribute forces on the patella. In severe cases, ice and anti-inflammatory medicine will be necessary to calm down inflammation before exercises can be initiated. Occasionally, a patella tracking brace or special taping techniques will be used.

Most patients will improve with nonsurgical management. In resistant cases arthroscopic surgery can be very helpful in smoothing out the roughened surface of the patella, removing any loose fragments of cartilage, and realigning the patella. Many cases of chondromalacia can be helped by a mini-arthroscopy performed under local anesthesia in the office.

Patella Malalignment

The normal patella should track straight down the middle of the femoral groove. There are varying degrees of abnormal tracking, or patella malalignment. In mild cases of malalignment the patella is simply tilted in the groove, leading to increased pressure on the downward tilted side of the patella.

Think of this as being like a tire out of alignment, where a subtle imbalance can quickly lead to uneven wear of the tire treads. In more severe cases, the patella will actually sublux or slide partially out of the groove. In the most severe cases of malalignment, the patella will completely dislocate.

Proper tracking of the patella is influenced by many factors. Good muscle balance is important and is one of the few factors one can control. Usually the patella wants to sublux toward the outside of the knee (lateral). Strengthening the inside muscle can counter this tendency.

Tracking is also influenced by the anatomical shape of your patella and femoral groove, the angle your knee makes with your hip (knock-knees), and even the position of your foot (pronation). The hip-knee angle is important because the patella is embedded in the quadriceps tendon that originates at the hip and attaches at the knee.

The more knock-kneed someone is, the more of an angular pull occurs on the patella every time the quadriceps contracts. This angle is called the Q angle. In severe cases of angulation (a high Q angle) surgery can be performed to correct the Q angle. The shape of the patella and femoral groove cannot be easily modified.

Increased pronation of the foot (flat feet) can influence the tracking of the patella. This occurs because the rotation of the rest of the leg is affected by the way the foot contacts the ground. Patients with increased pronation can use shoe orthotics (arch supports) that may help patella tracking by modifying the rotation of the knee.

Treatment Options: For severe cases of patella malalignment, arthroscopic surgery may be necessary. In the past, patients with an unstable patella were subjected to an extensive operative procedure that involved making an incision to tighten the inner ligaments controlling the tracking of the patella. The new arthroscopic method for realigning the patella has been used successfully for the past four years. So far, none of the patients has had any recurrent instability and all are extremely pleased with their surgical results. X-ray studies have confirmed the improvement in tracking of the patella.

An even newer technique for treatment of some types of patella instability is the use of a heated probe to shrink the stretched patella ligament. This method eliminates the need for any incisions or sutures in the knee and is currently being used for patients with less severe instability of the patella (subluxation).

Patella Dislocation

The patella is held in place by thin ligaments that act as reins, keeping it from coming out of the femoral groove, while the muscles provide the fine tuning. With severe twisting maneuvers or direct trauma, the patella can dislocate, tearing these ligaments and coming completely out of place.

If the patella spontaneously reduces, a trip to the emergency room may be necessary. Because the ligaments have torn, the patella usually will continue to be off balance even after the dislocation is reduced. This will lead to abnormal tracking and increased risk of dislocation in the future. In addition, small fragments of cartilage are often chipped off as the patella dislocates and can cause damage to the joint as they float around.

Numerous studies have shown that patients who have dislocated their patella do not do well in the long term, suffering repeated dislocations or developing degeneration under the kneecap due to the now-abnormal tracking. Recommended treatment is for immediate arthroscopic evaluation to remove the loose chips and to repair the torn ligaments and rebalance the patella tracking.

IF YOU'VE INJURED YOUR ANKLE

Recurring Sprains

Ankle sprains are extremely common. Typically the ankle will twist inward (invert) and the ligaments on the outside of the ankle will tear. The severity of the sprain depends on how much of the ligament tears, ranging from grade 1 (mild) to grade 3 (complete).

Treatment Options: Most people will heal after an ankle sprain and will be able to stabilize the joint and prevent recurring sprains with exercises and rehabilitation. A small percentage will suffer recurring sprains and the ankle will give out easily, often with a simple misstep while walking. In these cases surgery may be recommended to repair the torn ligaments. The most com-

ANKLE ARTHROSCOPY

Ankle arthroscopy allows athletes to return to sports rapidly. The most common indications for arthroscopy of the ankle follow:

- **Loose bodies:** Fragments of loose cartilage or bone are removed from the joint (common after multiple sprains).

- **Osteochondritis dissecans (OCD):** Damaged bone and cartilage on the talus bone of the ankle are treated by drilling deep into the bone to encourage bleeding and growth of healing cells.

- **Arthritis:** Loose debris and inflammatory enzymes are washed free. Spurs are removed.

- **Fusion:** In severe cases of arthritis, the joint can be fused arthroscopically.

- **Impingement:** Painful scar tissue that pinches in the front of the ankle is removed.

- **Fractures:** In some cases, splinters of bone are removed from the joint after fractures.

monly performed repair is called a Brostrom repair and involves the direct repair and tightening of the original ligament reinforced with other local tissue.

Osteochondritis Dissecans (OCD)

Osteochondritis dissecans (OCD) is a loss of blood supply to a segment of bone and cartilage in the talus bone of the ankle. Symptoms usually include pain in the inside corner of the joint. Often OCD cannot be detected with standard x-rays, and an MRI is necessary for diagnosis. The exact cause of OCD is not known, although a history of trauma is common.

Treatment Options: Occasionally in very young patients, OCD will heal with immobilization and rest. Most often it requires surgical treatment. Initial treatment involves arthroscopy to remove severely damaged fragments or to drill through the area with no blood supply into adjacent healthy bone. This allows blood supply to enter the injured area and encourage healing.

In severe cases, when drilling is not effective, a new procedure allows the transplantation of new cartilage and bone into the defect. A plug of cartilage and bone is taken from a safe area in the knee joint and implanted into the defective area in the ankle. Early results using this technique are very encouraging, with most patients achieving excellent relief of pain.

SPECIAL CONSIDERATIONS FOR THE FEMALE ATHLETE

While weight training and working out can benefit just about everyone, there are some special considerations Dr. Halbrecht has observed in female athletes.

Scoliosis

Scoliosis, or curvature of the spine, is much more common in females and tends to occur in adolescence. X-rays and medical evaluation will be necessary for diagnosis. Altered posture, particularly a difference in shoulder height or hip height, should raise concern.

Mitral Valve Prolapse

Mitral valve prolapse is a common, usually benign abnormality of one of the heart valves and occurs primarily in females. This is identified usually by a very specific type of murmur found on cardiac evaluation with a simple stethoscope. The majority of cases are asymptomatic and will not affect sports participation. Athletes with a history of fainting, arrhythmias, chest pain, or family history of heart disease should be referred for evaluation by a cardiologist.

Menstruation

Amenorrhea (lack of menstruation) should be identified as a flag for possible eating disorders and other problems.

Ligament Laxity

Females with excessive laxity of their ligaments should be advised that they may be at increased risk of knee, shoulder, and ankle injuries and should be particularly encouraged to participate in strengthening exercises to protect the joints. Additionally, certain findings might be useful in advising young females regarding choice of sport. For example, at an early age, females with hyperlax shoulders might be dissuaded from pursuing such sports as swimming or volleyball, and those with unstable patellas might be discouraged from running and twisting sports.

Spondylolysis

The young female gymnast or ballerina is particularly at risk for developing a spinal injury called spondylolysis, which is basically a stress fracture of the posterior elements of the spine. This is thought to result from the repetitive hyperextension required of these activities. Many of these athletes are also amenorrheic, making them more prone to develop stress fractures. The female athlete with localized back pain that does not resolve quickly should be referred for medical and x-ray evaluation.

Shin Splints

Exertional compartment syndrome is one of the causes of leg pain commonly known as shin splints. This form of shin splints occurs only during exercise and quickly resolves after activity ceases. In female athletes, the menstrual cycle and use of birth control pills can affect fluid shifts in the muscle compartments. In the female athlete suspected of having exertional compartment syndrome, modification of birth control medication may be curative.

ARE FEMALE ATHLETES REALLY DIFFERENT?

Certain physiological and sociological factors differentiate the female athlete. The sociological differences are based on generations of attitudes in society that create conflicting images for the young female. Although sports have become more accepted for girls, the media continues to bombard young women with the message that they also need to maintain a supermodel figure and a certain feminine image. These conflicting signals create significant stress for some females, causing eating disorders, which, along with certain physiological female traits, can combine to create a serious disorder called the female triad.

Physiologically, the female athlete has to deal with menstruation and hormonal balance. Stress, diet, over-training, and other factors can alter the normal menstrual cycle and hormonal balance, which can then affect the musculoskeletal system.

Anatomical Differences

Women can be just as competitive as men and can enjoy sports as much as men, but there are physiological and anatomical differences that affect these athletes. These include the following:

- **Strength:** Female athletes as a group are not as strong as their male counterparts. Studies have shown that with weight training, women will increase their strength percentagewise in equal increments to men, but their overall strength will begin and end at lower levels.
- **Speed:** Leg length in women is a smaller percentage of overall body length, which may be one reason that women tend to be slower runners than men.
- **Endurance:** Women seem to be approaching men in endurance performance much more rapidly than in strength or speed events. It is speculated that women may in fact be better suited physiologically to endurance activity than men due to an enhanced ability to conserve muscle glycogen and to use fat for energy, and therefore to more efficiently use oxygen.
- **Laxity:** Women tend to have more lax ligaments than males, which is thought to put their joints at increased risk for injury. A recent study has shown that the risk of injury in women may correlate to hormonal changes associated with the menstrual cycle. In particular, female athletes may be more prone to knee ligament injuries, shoulder instability, and ankle sprains.

Women's bodies are different from men's bodies in specific bodyparts, such as the following:

- **Hips and patella:** Women have wider hips than men, which creates a wider angle at the knee, where the kneecap (patella) articulates with the femur. This increased angle (Q angle) affects the tracking of the patella and predisposes the female athlete to tracking problems.

Abnormal tracking of the patella may lead to instability or dislocation of the patella, or simply cause pain due to unbalanced loading of the joint. The female athlete should emphasize strengthening exercises that stabilize the patella to help improve tracking and prevent injury. These exercises should focus on the inner quadriceps muscles.

- **ACL:** The female athlete seems to be disproportionately at risk for injury to the anterior cruciate ligament (ACL). There are several theories about the reasons for this increased risk. One is that because women tend to have a narrower space in the knee available for the ACL, less stress is required to tear the ligament than in the male athlete. A recent study has also shown that female athletes tend to rely on their quadriceps more than their hamstrings compared to their male counterparts. Because the hamstrings are one of the main protectors of the ACL, relative weakness in this structure may lead to ACL injuries. Additional risk of injury is related to estrogen levels.

Female athletes tend to sustain injury to the ACL during the ovulatory period of their menstrual cycle (generally around days 10 to 14). This is the period when estrogen levels are the highest. Researchers have shown that the ACL contains estrogen receptors and that the ACL responds to estrogen by decreasing cell activity and synthesis of the basic ligament fibers (collagen). Conditioning to build and maintain knee muscle strength, particularly the hamstrings, may help reduce the risk of injury.

- **Ankle and foot:** Female athletes have been shown to have a higher incidence of ankle sprains than males. This is most likely due to several factors, including increased ligamentous laxity and decreased muscle strength and coordination. Women also have a narrower heel in relation to the forefoot than men.

Strength and coordination exercises for the ankle are recommended to limit the risk of this injury. Use of a balance board and elastic bands for inversion and eversion exercises is particularly helpful.

Women tend to get bunions and hammertoes from narrow shoes. These can be painful and affect athletic performance. Wider athletic shoes and bunion pads may be helpful. Improved

shoes off the field may help prevent this problem.

- **Shoulder:** Increased ligament laxity may place the female athlete at higher risk for shoulder instability, particularly in sports that include overhead arm motions such as volleyball, tennis, swimming, and baseball. Women tend to have less upper-body strength than men as well, adding to the risk. Rotator cuff strengthening exercises may help to prevent this injury. Internal and external rotation exercises using elastic tubing with the arm at the side are particularly helpful.

APPENDIX B

For More Information

If you would like more information on the topics discussed in this book, you can contact the following professionals.

Ronnie Coleman
Big Ron, Inc.
2921 South Cooper Street, #109
Arlington, TX 76015
www.bigroncoleman.com or
    www.ronniecoleman.net

Ralph DeHann
www.ralphdehaanphotography.com

Christian Finn
www.thefactsaboutfitness.com or
    www.christianfinn.com

Jeffrey Halbrecht, M.D.
Institute for Arthroscopy and
    Sports Medicine
2100 Webster Street, Suite 331
San Francisco, CA 94115
Fax: 415-923-5896
Phone: 415-923-0944
www.iasm.com
jhalbrecht@iasm.com

Ken Lain
d.b.a. Barbell Ranch
3301 South 14th Street, Suite 45
Abilene, TX 79605
Phone: 915-691-0273
kslain@aol.com

Carol Semple
www.carolsemple.com